Quilt

YOUR STORY

Landauer Publishing

Quilt Your Story

Landauer Publishing, www.landauerpub.com, is an imprint of Fox Chapel Publishing Company, Inc.

Project Team
Managing Editor: Gretchen Bacon
Acquisitions Editor: Amelia Johanson
Editor: Christa Oestreich
Designer: Mary Ann Kahn
Studio Photographer: Mike Mihalo
Proofreader: Jeremy Hauck
Indexer: Jay Kreider

Shutterstock used: Gulcin Ragibogglu (22), VDB Photos (33 background), Rina Chypachenko (45 background), brizmaker (49 background, 69 background), T Cassidy (57 background), PopTika (61 background), Africa Studio (75 background, 77 background), Mateusz Gzik (87 background)

ISBN 978-1-63981-030-7

Library of Congress Control Number: 2023942300

We are always looking for talented authors. To submit an idea, please send a brief inquiry to acquisitions@foxchapelpublishing.com.

Note to Professional Copy Services:
The publisher grants you permission to make up to six copies of any quilt patterns in this book for any customer who purchased this book and states the copies are for personal use.

Printed in China
First printing

Quilt Your Story

Honoring Special Moments
Using Uniforms, Scrubs, Favorite Shirts, and More
to Make Memory Quilts and Projects

· · · · · · · · · · · · · · · · · · · ·

Kristin La Flamme

Contents

Introduction, 6

Getting Started, 8
  Organizing and Color Choices, 9
  Deconstructing and Preparing, 12
  Starting to Sew, 20

Memory Projects, 30
  Mike's Stars, 32
    Mike's Story, 32
    Log Star Pillow, 34
    Anvil Star Pillow, 37
    Sawtooth Star Pillow, 38
    Variation: Scrappy Star Quilt, 42

  Ralph's Square Dance, 44
    Ralph's Story, 44
    Square Dance Quilt, 46

  Gregory's Wonky Stars, 48
    Gregory's Story, 48
    Wonky Star Quilt, 50
    Variation: HST Throw Pillow, 54

  Kenny's Stripes, 56
    Kenny's Story, 56
    Stripes Quilt, 58

  Joni's Pathway, 60
    Joni's Story, 60
    Pathway Table Runner, 62
    Variation: Patio Pillow, 66

  Angela's Aspens, 68
    Angela's Story, 68
    Aspens Quilt, 70

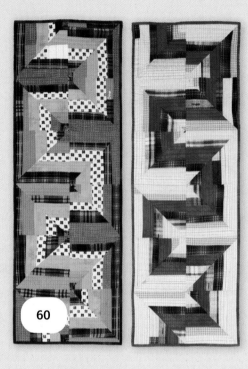

  Constanze's Textile Art, 72
    Constanze's Story, 72
    Flock Wall Art, 74
    Hearth Wall Art, 76
    Arcs Wall Art, 79
    Grow Wall Art, 81
    Waterfall Wall Art, 83
    Art's Story, 84

  Art's Portal, 86
    Art's Story, 86
    Portal Quilt, 88

  Eden's Cairn, 90
    Eden's Story, 90
    Cairn Table Runner, 92
    Variation: Small Cairn Quilt, 98

  Katja's Froggy Monster, 100
    Katja's Story, 100
    Froggy-Monster Backpack, 102
    Variation: Just a Stuffie, 107

  Tanner's Patchwork, 110
    Tanner's Story, 110
    Patchwork Tote, 112

Gallery, 115

Index, 119

About the Author, 120

86

56

44

110

100

90

Introduction

Tribute. Honor. Comfort. A memory quilt is so much more than just a cozy bed covering—it warms the heart and soul. Each of the projects ahead will share a unique quilt or quilted project and the story of the person whom it was made for, followed by instructions on how to make your own version or variation. There is a range of projects, including large bed quilts, snuggle quilts, and wall art, as well as smaller items for when you have less fabric or time—or when you want to keep going!

Creating a quilt from special fabrics steeped in sentiment is powerful yet often fraught with its own set of challenges. Where do you start? How do you incorporate disparate materials? How do you honor those materials? How do you turn clashing or dull-colored or mundane (yet meaningful) uniforms into something both stylish and thoughtful? For the quilts and projects in this book, I used solid colors as a backdrop to unify (or ground) the special fabrics I chose to highlight. Using a combination of minimal colors and uncomplicated designs works well with a wide variety of materials and simplifies the process so that you can be confident in the finished product, even if you are not a confident designer yourself. The project patterns are purposefully simple to highlight the special fabrics within and to be approachable for quilters from confident beginner onward, leaving you to get straight to the making part of creating a special quilt to cherish.

When we were newlyweds, my husband joined the army, and we embarked on what would become 20 years of worldwide travels and adventures. His career included peacekeeping missions in Bosnia–Herzegovina and Kosovo as well as four tours in Iraq. With all those years, deployments, and locations came multiple uniforms of various colors and patterns. What creative quilter could ignore that growing pile of fabric? Each uniform signified not only a stage in his career, but also carried memories to be honored. I wanted to do more than store one of each in a trunk, only to be taken out on Memorial Day, if at all.

Little by little, the uniforms made their way into my artwork, helping to tell my story of life as an army wife. From these textiles, I created a series of artworks in the form of quilts, apron forms, and even a 3D sculpture. The work has been therapeutic for me, and through it, I have spoken to many other spouses who were able to see a little of themselves in my narratives. That interaction seeded an idea to find a way to incorporate uniforms into something beautiful, useful, and meaningful; and one that I could make for, and with, others. To embrace a wider audience, this book has grown to include ideas for a variety of sentimental fabrics—not just uniforms.

So, what is your story?

Getting Started

Starting your memory quilt can be challenging or intimidating. You have a person, place, or event you want to honor. But where do you start? Maybe it's easy—a pile of your dad's favorite shirts, the scrubs you wore during your residency, or the T-shirts from four years of high school drama club. But maybe it's a closet full of keepsakes, and you're not sure if it all works together. The following are simple ways to look at your collection and determine how it might fit together. The number or size of garments or other special fabrics will help determine what size project you'll want to make. Check the patterns for estimates. Stay flexible.

Organizing and Color Choices

You have a pile of sentimental garments or other textiles. Now what? How do you unify a potentially disparate collection of garments or other special fabrics? Here are a few options to think about.

Flannel shirts (top) match well despite the range of colors, especially when there is a bit of one color running through the collection. Ties (bottom) can make for a great collection.

Picking one color, such as red (top), can unite a collection of fabrics, but don't be afraid to use mostly one color with an accent, such as blue with pink (bottom).

Sort by Type

It can be helpful to group items by type, such as just flannel shirts or just ties. But don't be too strict—denim jeans mixed in with T-shirts adds texture and contrast.

Consider that the items don't all need to come from the same person. How about a wedding quilt made from a shirt contributed by each member of the wedding party (best to coordinate on a basic color) or an anniversary quilt with garments from many family members?

Sort by Color

My favorite way to pull things together is with color. Start by pinning your garments and any other special fabrics to the wall, or laying them on a table or floor, to give you an idea of how they work together. Is there a dominant color? Maybe they are all warm reds to browns, or mostly blues and greens? Are they neutrals, or are they a riot of bright colors? If the collection feels cohesive, you are ready to choose an accent fabric. Does the recipient, or person honored in the piece, have a favorite color? That can be inspiration for your accent—how does it look with your collection?

You might discover that most of your fabrics are dark, which can create interesting contrast with a light accent fabric (or vice versa).

Sort by Contrast

What if the collection still feels jumbled? Try taking out a piece. Or try arranging the materials from light to dark. Are they mostly lights? Or mostly darks? Picking something very light to show off a dark collection of special fabrics, or dark against a mostly light collection, will bring together a varied palette. The background for Gregory's Wonky Stars quilt needed to be light so that the richly colored flannel stars would show up. I chose gray, but a creamy color would have worked well too. Garments of many bright colors will hold together when mixed with one dark, or very light, accent. Light shirts will read as cohesive when paired with one medium or dark color. A neutral or contrasting accent puts the focus on the special fabrics.

Adding an Accent Color

Once you have decided which quilt or project to make and organized your special fabrics, it's time to choose your accent(s). All the projects in this book suggest using one or more accent color of a purchased fabric to unite your special fabrics. Your choice of accent fabric will ground a collection by providing contrast or tying it all together. Your accent color can even be a neutral or old jeans (they go with everything, right?). This is what will keep the piece cohesive. Using a few solid fabrics, or near solids, will pull together the colors or ideas of your special fabrics.

Adding a solid color to a group of patterns is a great start. I like how this warm orange contrasts the cool, dark colors in this collection.

When I approach a quilt accent, my first thought is usually to try to highlight a color already in the collection. Maybe there's green in a plaid, a graphic on a tee, or the color of a pair of pants. Use that color as your accent to tie it all together. We're not necessarily looking for "matchy-matchy" but something in the same color family. Maybe there's rusty, or red, stripes repeating in several fabrics. Maybe most of the T-shirt graphics include yellow. Look for a color in the tiny details of the fabrics you use.

If I'm not inspired by the options already in the fabric, I then consider making my accent a complementary color: a red or pink to accent a greenish collection, golden tones to accent purply colors, or peachy-orange to accent blues. (As an aside, purples and greens always look good together—it's a rule my friend Deborah follows to great effect.)

If you have a stash of plain-colored fabric, use it to audition colors. Maybe you already have the perfect piece! You can also gather a variety of swatches from the paint aisle at your local home-improvement store and use them to try out color combos before heading to the fabric store—especially if you decide to shop online. I find, though, that there is no substitute for taking your pile of special fabrics to the fabric store and holding them next to various bolts of potential colors. Many shop employees love putting color combos together and will be happy to help you.

The yellows and greens were too much variety for these mostly blue fabrics used in Pathway Table Runner. When I removed them and settled on the lime green accent, the collection sang.

Finally, take notes so you don't forget what colors you want to use where—especially if you plan to deviate from the basic pattern. For example, you may want to use special fabrics in place of one or two accent fabrics for the Sawtooth Star Pillow. For Constanze's Flock Wall Art, I used her blue shirt in place of an accent fabric as it was solid colored and coordinated perfectly with her other fabrics. Notes will help you stay organized and on track.

Some of my favorite accent fabrics are solids, such as Kona® by Robert Kaufman Fabrics. Grunge by Moda Fabrics seems to work with just about everything too. Palette by Windham Fabrics and Shadow Play by Maywood Studio has a nice subtle patterning that reads solid but isn't boring. Burlap by Benartex is a classic with just enough visual texture to be interesting. Shot cottons (where the warp and weft threads are different colors) are beautiful, if a little more wiggly to work with. Keep your purchased accent fabric simple so that your special fabrics are the stars!

Above are some of my go-to solids and near solids. They provide balance to the piece without taking focus away from the beloved garments and other special fabrics.

Deconstructing and Preparing

The next step is the hardest: cutting up that special fabric! First, read the pattern requirements for the project you want to sew. The special fabric needs that are listed will be approximate, but they will give you a basic idea for whether you need to use an entire garment or just a part of it. With a basic plan in mind for what you will need from each piece of clothing, you are ready to deconstruct.

Identify any elements that you would like to highlight. Patches and pockets can be removed, or stay as design elements. I often remove patches and name tags. After quilting, I reapply them in different positions. Or I tuck an element like a tag or a belt loop into a seam as I sew. It might be desirable to remove a pocket or open a seam to show fading or patina (as in Kenny's Arcs Wall Art on page 118), but otherwise, I usually don't bother. It's also fun to cut around a pocket and use that piece for something like a star center, such as in the Anvil Star pillow.

Notes About Deconstructing Clothing

To begin, choose how much deconstructing you want to do. Some people like to completely deconstruct a piece of clothing as an act of respect, to get the most out of it, or to uncover interesting details. It is not always necessary to do this, though you are more than welcome to. You can also choose to cut only the focus of your fabric, such as the logo on a T-shirt or the patch on a jacket. Regardless of how much deconstructing you plan to do, the fabric is much easier to work with when it is no longer in garment form and it lies flat. Once deconstructed, you can treat it like yardage.

To fully deconstruct a garment, use a seam ripper and go slowly to avoid poking a hole where you don't want one. It is often easier to see the stitches you want to "rip" on the back side of the fabric. I also use my 8" (20.3cm) dressmaker's scissors to cut the garment apart.

If you are going to use only a specific element from a garment, just rough-cut the element from the chosen area, about 1" (2.5cm) larger all around. No need to deconstruct further.

Remove buttons to avoid accidentally hitting them when quilting. Patches can be removed if they are not already in an optimal placement. When your quilting is finished, then you can add any buttons, pins, and patches back on by hand or machine. If making a pillow, add these before assembling the front to the back of the pillow.

The deconstructing process is an opportunity to commune with the garment and think about the person or event it represents. Memory quilts are meditations, not races to the finish line. Do remain flexible, because sometimes we inadvertently cut or rip holes in places that we didn't mean to.

You have the option of only using part of your garment. Here are some examples of rough-cut details from T-shirts, jeans, and a onesie.

Order of Operations

The patterns in this book jump right into cutting and sewing pieces because you may be using different fabrics than I did for my quilts. This section covers what you need to do before starting the project. Make sure you complete these steps:

1. **Deconstruct your garments.** If needed, rough-cut the desired parts, at least 1" (2.5cm) larger all around.

2. **Remove buttons, patches, pins, etc. that could get in the way of sewing or quilting.** When your quilting is finished, you can then add them back on.

3. **Stabilize your special fabrics if you need to.** Don't forget any rough-cut pieces that may also need stabilizing.

4. **Prepare the pattern pieces according to the project.**

   Example 1: Rough-cut the large motif on the back of a T-shirt. Then rough-cut the small motif on the front. Cut either 1" or 2" (2.5 or 5.1cm) larger than you will need for the pattern. Stabilize those with your interfacing, then cut them to the size required in the pattern.

   Example 2: Cut the back and two fronts from a flannel shirt. Dampen them with Terial Magic or starch. Let them dry. Iron. Cut the pieces required for the pattern. This way, you don't waste product on shirt parts like sleeves that you won't be using, and your product will go further.

For Shirts

Shirts are the most common garments to transform into a memory quilt because they often feature a logo, print, embroidered detail, or patch that holds sentimental value. Sometimes, you may just want to save that specific feature without the rest of the shirt; in this case, rough cutting will be your best option. However, if you want to keep the entire shirt to use as yardage, it's important to cut the pieces apart to get the most out of them.

Rough Cutting

1. Determine what you will be cutting. Most of your pieces will be used as a quilt block or a unit within a block. Check what size you need before cutting because you may need more fabric around the featured section than expected. Spread out your shirt as flat as possible. Lay the appropriate square quilt ruler over the logo, making sure it is centered. If your quilt ruler is too large, use tape to block off the size required. Trace with a marking pen or chalk.

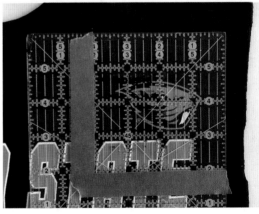

2. Mark the seam allowance. Place a ruler ¼" (6mm) away from the line you traced and draw with a marking pen or chalk. Repeat on all four sides.

3. Rough-cut around the lines. Use scissors to cut 1"–2" (2.5–5.1cm) around the traced area. You can then cut to size when cutting your pattern pieces.

Rough Cutting Options

Cutting a square with the logo centered may be the most common form of rough cutting, but it's not the only way to take advantage of your shirts. Here are a few variations that could inspire your projects and jazz up your blocks.

Cut off center. Your special design doesn't have to be centered in the block. In fact, many logos and embroidered details are placed on the left chest, making them hard to center. However, this can be turned into a design choice, drawing the eye to a unique spot on your quilt. You can also sew matching or coordinating strips of fabric around your logo until the desired size is reached. I find this works best for smaller designs, but see what you prefer.

Cut a rectangle or strip. You will quickly discover that many logos aren't square or easy to cut into a block. However, these garments shouldn't be disregarded. "Blocks" aren't necessarily square. Many projects in this book, such as Kenny's Stripes and Katja's Froggy Monster, take advantage of unique shapes to show them off beautifully. Remember that you don't have to keep designs intact. Cutting Kenny's car shirts into strips creates a colorful rhythm across the quilt, even though you don't see a whole car.

Smaller logos can be used for both large and small blocks.

You could leave this as a rectangle, but this design could be split into two squares.

Deconstructing Shirts

1. Cut off collars and cuffs. Follow the seam lines with your scissors to preserve the shape in case you want to use these pieces. Cut along the side seams until you reach the armhole.

2. Cut around the armhole on each side of the seam. Cut down the sleeve seam to open the fabric. Cut the shoulder seams to separate the front and back.

3. Lay out your pieces to see how you want to use them. You can keep a shirt front intact and use it for a pillow back. If I don't need to save the whole shirt front, I almost always cut off and save the shirt buttons for use elsewhere.

For Pants

1. Cut the legs off below the pockets. Set this piece aside for rough-cutting the details. If you prefer, leave the whole leg intact and cut off the waistband, then continue.

2. Open the leg. Cut on both sides of the thick inseam. Cut along the side seam. I may use my seam ripper to open the side seam and hem. You can also use your rotary cutter and mat for the job—whatever feels most comfortable to you.

3. Rough-cut specific pockets, labels, or other details. On a flat garment, I often save pockets for incorporating into a pattern piece. Make sure to leave at least 1" (2.5cm) all around the piece for cutting and seam allowances.

4. Optionally, cut these details out. You may want to appliqué a label or apply a pocket separately. I use a seam ripper for these tasks to ensure nothing is destroyed.

For Other Garments

For most garments, opening or removing seams and hems is enough. But for garments like uniforms that have lots of pockets, or if you want to squeeze every last bit of fabric out of a piece, you may need to deconstruct even more. This uniform jacket is an example.

1. Cut on each side of the seams as you would with other garments. I broke this jacket into two sleeves and several long strips that made up the front and back.

2. Cut off collars and cuffs. This can be done before step 1 if you prefer; however, I like to focus on the larger pieces first with unusual garments.

3. Remove pockets and belt loops with a seam ripper. This will expose more structural seams and provide extra fabric.

4. Once pockets are removed, open the once-covered seams. Rather than going around pockets, you can now use as much fabric as provided.

Yardage Uses

Once deconstruction is complete, it is time to cut your pattern pieces. I always start with the largest pieces or the pieces with a specific element, such as a design or pocket. As much as possible, try to cut your shapes on grain—the straight sides should be parallel to the threads of the special fabric. Follow your notes and the pattern to cut the necessary pieces for your project.

Here are some options to keep in mind:

- **Use the shirt front.** Buttons, snaps, and tassels may not be an obvious choice for creating a quilt, but they make for a unique and beloved feature on a favorite shirt. Incorporating the closure or front details gives a personal touch. Use the front as a block for a pillow or quilt, such as Angela's Aspens. I recommend removing the buttons as you work to avoid catching them on your machine, then adding them back on at the end.

- **Use multiple pieces.** The process of deconstructing can leave you with some strange shapes, and not all of them are useful on their own. Remember, it is also acceptable to sew two smaller pieces together and then cut out your desired larger piece, especially if the pieces are of a similar color and value.

- **Use for patchwork piecing.** Just like quilting cotton, you can use your smaller bits of fabric for piecing. Make a patchwork of fabric squares, turn them into HSTs, or incorporate them into larger designs like the big rectangles in Angela's Aspens.

- **Use for specialty piecing.** There are more than squares in quilting! Whether you are making curved blocks or doing English paper piecing, you can cut up your special fabrics into anything you can imagine. To achieve this, however, you might need to cut into a larger design. The idea of cutting into a logo might not be appealing to you, but it makes for a very modern and interesting piece. For Eden's Cairn, the unique shapes broke up some T-shirt logos, but there were still readable elements.

This shirt might pass for normal fabric until you notice the buttons, which makes for a special touch to your piece.

Your special garments can be featured as both large and small pieces. This way, you can incorporate even more throughout a quilt.

Selecting parts of a logo to cut out can make for a big impact, such as highlighting "all our lives" in this scrub top.

Fabric Prep

Some of your fabrics may need a little extra preparation before you use them in a quilt or other project to make them easier to sew together.

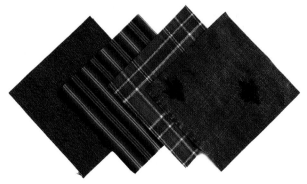

Medium-weight cottons and denim. Usually, medium-weight cottons (such as dress shirts), denim, and canvas only need pressing before cutting pattern pieces. Use a pressing cloth between your iron and the fabric.

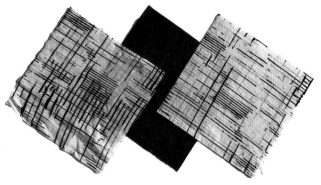

Delicate fabrics. Threadbare or very lightweight fabrics (such as ties, delicate cottons, and rayons) need a stabilizer fused to the back side to prevent distortion of the weave. This will make the fabric easier to work with and ease frustration. The left swatch is not stabilized, the right is.

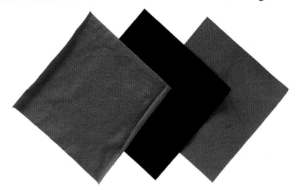

Stretchy fabrics. You may encounter a variety of stretchy fabrics, such as T-shirt and fashion knits. They all should be stabilized before cutting to final size. Stabilizer will prevent the pieces from stretching and rolling (like the left swatch) as you sew them together—therefore avoiding distortion.

Adding Interfacing

There are two main ways for stabilizing fabric: liquid stabilizer and fusible interfacing. Both are easy to apply, though interfacing may not be as intuitive. Here is what you need to know.

1. Place interfacing on the wrong side of the fabric. Your piece should be just as large or larger than the fabric area you are cutting. Press the layers with an iron for about 10 seconds. Lift and move to another section; only lift and press the iron.

2. Cut excess stabilizer. Here, I cut the lower-left corner that was hanging off the fabric. The stabilized area of your garment can now be cut for pattern pieces.

Stabilizers for Delicate or Stretchy Fabrics

- **Pellon® SF101 Shape-Flex® fusible interfacing**. Woven. Good for delicates like ties and very thin cottons. I think it has too much body and weight for T-shirt quilts, but others love the stability it provides.

- **Pellon 906F Fusible Sheerweight interfacing**. Easy to use. Excellent for thin fashion knits, often used for T-shirt quilts. Adds a little weight.

- **Pellon EK130 Easy Knit™ fusible interfacing**. Easy to use. Good for T-shirt quilts and fashion fabrics. Adds a little weight.

- **Touch O' Gold II fusible interfacing**. Fiddly. Needs sharp tools. Excellent drape. Still stretchy. Use a walking foot and caution.

- **Spray starch**. Good for linens and medium-weight cottons. It adds just enough stability to make cutting and sewing more accurate. Washes out when the project is complete.

Use a sink to soak your fabrics in liquid stabilizers to make the cleanup easier.

- **Liquid starch**. Not as ubiquitous as it used to be, but a less-expensive alternative to Terial Magic. Use at full strength or dilute two parts starch to one part water. Good for T-shirts and flannel garments to avoid distortion when cutting and sewing. Washes out when the project is complete.

- **Terial Magic**. Makes fabric stiff but washes out soft. It has enough of a scent that I'd caution against using it if you have a sensitive nose. A 16 oz. bottle is enough to dampen three to four large T-shirts.

From left to right: Fabric with interfacing added, starched fabric, and a swatch without any stabilizing. You can see the huge difference that stabilizing makes.

Starting to Sew

This book assumes you have done some sewing already and have a sewing machine on which you are able to sew a consistent, straight seam allowance. The information here will focus on the tools and techniques you will need to successfully complete the projects in this book.

Supplies

Some basic supplies from the quilting world are all you need to create the projects in this book. You probably already have most of the items listed at hand. The better the quality, the more use you will get out of them—for these projects and beyond. I've listed my favorites that I can't live (or sew) without.

Must-Have Supplies

- **Sewing machine.** It's important use a machine in good working order when using special fabrics. Your machine doesn't need to be fancy (though I love the convenience features on my upscale machine). If you can, it's helpful to get to know your local dealer for service and education to keep your machine running smoothly, and so you can take advantage of all its features.

Don't skimp on the quality of sewing machine needles and threads—invest in the best products you can afford so that they will last longer and work better.

- **Machine feet.** For most of the projects in this book, all you really need is a machine that can sew a straight line. But specialty feet like a Zipper Foot, ¼" (6mm) Foot (sometimes called a Patchwork Foot), and Walking Foot (or the equivalent, as different manufacturers often use different terms) will help you sew more easily and accurately.

- **Quality thread.** The cheaper the thread, the more lint and lumpiness it can have, which can give your sewing machine fits. Gutermann and Mettler brands are good. I also very much like the brands Aurifil, Superior, and Quilters Select.

- **Sewing machine needle.** Start each project with a fresh needle. It's an inexpensive way to avoid false starts and skipped stitches. I usually use a SCHMETZ Microtex or sharp size 80, but I switch to a size 90 or 100 needle to sew through thick layers. Particularly thick patches with VELCRO® backs may even need a titanium-coated needle.

- **Iron and ironing board.** Pressing is your friend. Your iron does not need to be fancy, but it should be nearby!

- **Rotary cutter.** Use one with a fresh blade. I like a 45mm cutter with a squeeze handle or other easy way to cover the blade when I'm not using it. (I'm the one in the classroom who sheathes everyone's blades the minute they are done cutting.) Also, every time I change my blade, I wonder why I didn't do it sooner. A new, sharp blade is particularly nice when cutting pieces out of thicker garments like jeans and wool shirts.

- **6" x 24"** (15.2 x 61cm) **rotary ruler.** A rotary ruler is a thick, plastic straight edge to guide the blade of your rotary cutter. The rulers are marked in increments to help you cut the correct-size pieces from your fabric. They come in many sizes and some even have nonskid dots or coating on the back, which is great for keeping the ruler in place as you cut. If I could only ever have one ruler, this size would be it.

Both scissors and seam rippers are best for deconstructing clothes; rotary cutters, quilt rulers, and cutting mats are perfect for cutting purchased fabric and clothes after deconstruction.

- **Self-healing rotary mat.** 18" x 24" (45.7 x 61cm) or larger. 24" x 36" (61 x 91.4cm) is best but not essential.

- **Scissors.** The sharper the better. You will do much of your garment deconstructing with scissors. 8" (20.3cm) dressmaker's shears are the most universal. I like the brands KAI and Gingher. In addition, you might also like 6" (15.2cm) embroidery scissors, such as Karen Kay Buckley's Perfect Scissors™.

- **Seam ripper.** A seam ripper is great for removing buttons. It's also essential for redoing the sewing mistakes we *all* make.

- **Straight pins.** Pins are your friends; use as many as necessary to hold things in place. I am partial to the glass-head ones.

- **Pencil or chalk for marking.** I often use a #2 pencil for light-colored fabrics. A Clover Chaco chalk liner is another favorite as it brushes off easily. Even a sliver of white soap is a surprisingly good marking tool.

- **Press cloth.** A ⅓ yard (30.5cm) piece of muslin works great. Use a press cloth when ironing stabilizer or interfacing to the backs of delicate or stretchy fabrics. It seems like a hassle, but the bottom of your iron will thank you later, and it avoids accidentally melted interfacing too.

Optional Supplies

- **6½" x 6½"** (16.5 x 16.5cm) **Bloc Loc HST ruler.** Handy for squaring up half-square triangle (HST) blocks.

- **20"** (50.8cm) **square ruler.** Handy for fussy cutting motifs like T-shirt backs or embroideries.

- **Embroidery thread.** If you want to add some hand-embroidered details, then I recommend perle cotton thread. You can also use cotton embroidery floss or perle cotton for quilting or tying your project (page 28).

- **Glue.** For most projects, preferably use a glue stick made specially for fabric as they are smaller and wash away easily, but a regular glue stick will also work. You will also need tacky glue or a hot-glue gun for mounting onto canvas.

There are products designed specifically to work on fabric, but don't underestimate the basics like pencils and pens for your work as well.

Terms

Batting: The filler or middle layer of the quilt.

Bias: Refers to the diagonal direction across the vertical and horizontal grain of the fabric. You can also think of it as being 45 degrees from the selvage. Cuts on the bias are stretchier than cuts in the same direction as the threads of the fabric and should be handled with care when piecing a quilt.

Binding: A strip of fabric used to encase the edges of a quilted piece after the top, batting, and backing have been stitched together. It finishes the outer edge so the fabrics don't fray and the batting doesn't leak out of the edges.

Block: A design unit (usually a square) that is repeated to make a quilt top.

Border: The outer area of a quilt, much like a frame on a picture. A quilt can have multiple borders. A border tends to give a traditional look to a quilt (Gregory's Wonky Star quilt has both a narrow and a wider border), but not all quilts need a border (Kenny's Stripes quilt has no border).

Grain: The direction of the lengthwise and crosswise threads that make up the fabric.

HST: Half-Square Triangle. A quilting term for a square block made of two triangles.

Piecing: The act of stitching fabric pieces together to make a quilt top.

Quilt: Broadly, a layer-and-stitched construction. Most often refers to a bed covering made of three layers (backing, batting, and quilt top) stitched together for stability and bound on the edges.

Quilt top: The decorative side of a quilt, usually made of fabric pieces sewn together before it is layered with the backing and batting.

Quilt sandwich: Refers to the three layers of a quilt (backing, batting, and top) before being quilted and bound.

Quilting: The stitching that holds the quilt's three layers together. Quilting adds texture and design to the quilt.

Sashing: Strips of fabric sewn between blocks, also called lattice strips.

Seam: The line of stitching that joins two fabric pieces or other parts of a quilt.

Seam allowance: The fabric between the seam line and the cut edge. Seam allowances for quilt piecing are usually ¼" (6mm) wide.

Selvage: These are the long "self-finished" edges of the fabric that don't unravel. They can be of a different weave or thickness than the rest of the fabric, so are typically trimmed off when cutting pieces for quilting.

Template: A pattern around which seam lines or cutting lines are marked on fabric. Templates can be made from thin cardboard or see-through plastic.

WOF: Width of Fabric. This is the length from one selvage edge to the opposite selvage edge.

Techniques

The projects in this book don't go into detail for all the quilt basics being used. Those who are still beginning their quilting journey, or want a refresher, will find it handy to review these techniques and tips before jumping into a quilt.

Seam Allowance

Achieving an accurate ¼" (6mm) seam allowance is important no matter what kind of quilt you are making. What isn't always explained is that it's not just about sewing a straight line. The weight of your thread as well as the fabric you are using can affect your seam allowance. When making memory quilts with a variety of materials, it is important to test the accuracy of your seam allowance before diving into making the project.

Leaders and Enders

Nontraditional fabrics can be tricky; they can be stretchy, heavy, thick, thin, etc. Sometimes they are easily pushed down into the needle plate when you start sewing. Use leaders and enders as a strategy to prevent fabric from getting pushed into the needle plate or caught under the presser foot when starting. This tool is simply two layers of scrap fabric that you put under your presser foot when you start sewing.

Sew right off the edge of this "leader" and onto your quilt piece. Snip the scrap leader apart from your quilt piece whenever it's convenient. If desired, chain-piece (see page 24) more pieces. When you are done, sew off the last pair and onto your scrap (now it's called an "ender"). Snip the ender apart from the chain of pieces.

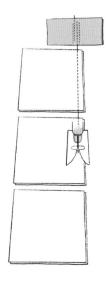

The leader (in gray) allows your machine to get started on a scrap piece of fabric before continuing onto your specialty pieces.

Check Your Seam Allowances

Cut two 2½" x 2½" (6.4 x 6.4cm) squares out of the fabric you plan to use. Sew the two pieces together with a ¼" (6mm) seam allowance and press the seam to one side. Now measure the finished piece. If it is 4½" (11.4cm) wide, then your machine settings are appropriate. If your piece is wider or narrower than 4½" (11.4cm), you will need to adjust your sewing machine settings.

Using a ¼" (6mm) foot allows you to line up the fabric along the edge of the foot to maintain consistency. You can also place washi tape or the Qtools Sewing Edge to align your fabric the necessary distance from the needle. If you have a computerized machine, there is probably a ¼" (6mm) setting, but you can also use your stitch width adjustment to move the needle even further to the right for the best scant ¼" (6mm) seam. You may prefer using a ¼" (6mm) foot to get the perfect seam size, or maybe it's easier to adjust your needle position. Experiment and find what works best for **you**. There is no single best way to set your ¼" (6mm) seam, only the way that works best for you, your fabric, and your sewing machine.

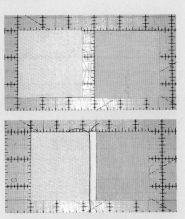

Tape, such as washi tape, is a cheap and easy way to ensure straight and even seam allowances.

Chain Piecing

Chain piecing is an efficient way to sew. In quilt making, it comes in handy in two ways. First is in sewing single units together, such as two squares in a Wonky Star block or making HSTs. The second way is in sewing your quilt blocks together, as it keeps all your pieces in the proper order when sewing the rows and columns. Sew without trimming the threads or removing them from the machine.

Units

Sew the first pieces. If making HSTs, sew ¼" (6mm) away from the marked line as shown. Continue to the next by sewing off the end of one pair and sewing onto the next pair without removing any pieces from the machine. When all the pieces have been sewn, snip the thread chain apart.

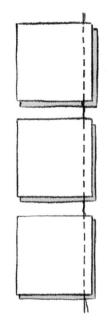

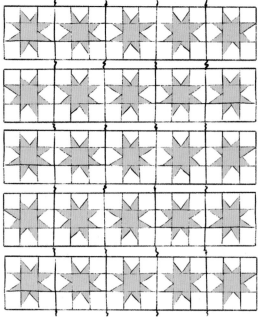

2. Go back to the first pair and sew on the third block from the first row. Without cutting the thread, continue to the second row and sew on the next block. Continue with the rest of the rows and cut the thread at the end. Each row will dangle from the previous row by the uncut "chain" threads. Press the rows as indicated in the pattern and then sew the rows together. Cut the chain threads and press the seams as indicated in the pattern.

Blocks

1. Lay out all your blocks in the desired order. Start with the upper-left block, and sew it to the next block to its right in the first row. Without taking those pieces out of the sewing machine, continue by sewing the first block in the second row to the next block to the right in the second row. Continue with the rest of the rows. This will connect the block pairs with a vertical thread chain. After the last pair, cut the thread.

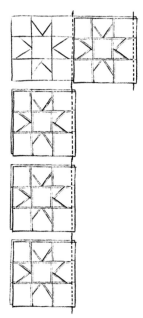

Nesting Seams

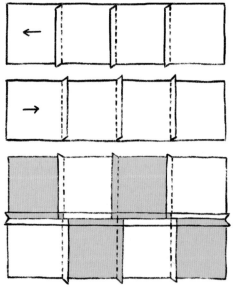

1. Press seam allowances in opposite directions on each row. This allows them to abut, or lock into, each other. It both reduces bulk and helps to create accurate intersections of your blocks.

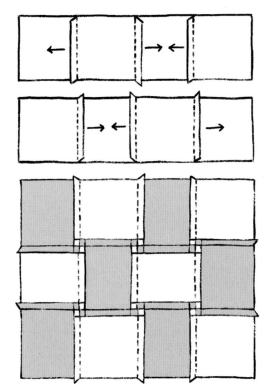

2. Take this even further by "twirling" the intersections for a flatter quilt top. Press rows in alternating pairs. This will result in two outer edges of the block having the seam allowances facing away from the center, and two opposite edges with seams facing toward the center. When sewing the rows of blocks together, the seams should nest. Open the intersections and press the horizontal seams in alternating directions. This process takes more time, but the result is an evenly flat quilt top.

Half-Square Triangles

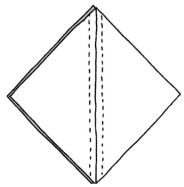

1. Draw a diagonal line on the back of one square from each pair to be used. It should be drawn from one corner to the opposite corner. Pair two squares, right sides together. Stitch ¼" (6mm) on each side of the drawn line for every pair. Pin perpendicular to the diagonal line. You can use the chain-piecing technique for this.

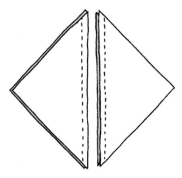

2. Cut on the drawn line. This will create two HST blocks from each pair.

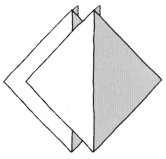

3. Press the seams to the darker fabric. Trim each HST block to square if necessary (the Bloc Loc ruler is very handy here).

Basting

If you are quilting on your domestic sewing machine or by hand, you will need to baste your three layers together. This a temporary hold, compared to the permanent connection done by quilting. There are many ways this can be achieved.

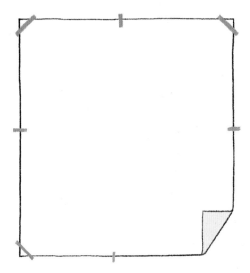

1. Lay the backing fabric face down. Tape it to the floor with painter's tape. Make sure it is smooth and a little taut, but not stretched. Lightly spray the backing with basting spray.

2. Smooth out the batting on top of the backing. Start at the center and work your way out to the edges.

3. Lay the quilt top face up on the batting. I don't spray-baste the top, but many do. Again, smooth from the center out.

4. Choose the basting technique of your choice. I typically use one of the options described on the right: pin basting and thread basting.

Pin Basting

This is my favorite way of basting. Use curved basting pins to hold the layers together. Work from the center out and place pins about a hand's width apart. Remove the tape. Quilt as desired, taking out the pins as you reach them.

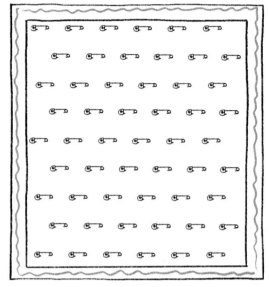

Pin Basting Diagram

Thread Basting

Basting can also be done with a needle and thread. Start from the center and take large (about 1" [2.5cm] long) stitches through all three layers, working your way out to the edges. You don't need to knot the thread; make

Thread Basting Diagram

a few small stitches in place when starting and ending. Remove tape.

I have also used a long-armer to baste a large quilt that I then hand-quilted. It is much less expensive to have a long-armer baste your quilt than to actually quilt it. You can then finish the quilt on your domestic machine or hand-quilt it. Have the long-armer use a water-soluble thread to baste, and it will disappear the first time you wash the finished quilt.

Quilting

Quilting, at its essence, means to hold two or more layers together with stitching. Typically, a quilt consists of a backing (usually one large piece of fabric, but often multiple pieces sewn together), batting, and the pieced quilt top, all held together with stitching. Each pattern advises you to construct your "sandwich" (putting together a backing, batting, and quilt top) and quilt as desired.

There are as many ways to quilt a project as there are quilters. In this book, I've used several different ways of quilting. Feel free to use the quilting technique that makes sense to you, your tools, and the project itself. For the projects in this book, I've used all-over machine quilting, tied embroidery floss at 2" (5.1cm) intervals, and hand quilting with large stitches and thick thread. Feel free to choose whichever suits your needs.

Straight-Line Quilting with a Walking Foot

Notice the navy thread being stitched in vertical lines along this project. Painter's tape helps to keep these lines straight and an equal distance apart.

This is a great way for you to quilt a smallish project on your home sewing machine. A walking foot moves the top layer of fabric in much the same way as the feed dogs move the bottom layer of fabric. Many sewing machines come with a walking foot, but if yours did not, your local sewing machine dealer can help you find the right one for your machine.

With the walking foot properly placed on your machine, increase the stitch length a few millimeters and plan your path. Depending on the design, I like to stitch down the center and then across the width. Then I work my way out to the edges. I often use blue painter's tape as a guide to sew next to, which keeps my lines straight and equidistant from each other. Something as simple as straight horizontal lines is very effective, especially in a small project like a pillow or a table runner. Success with a smaller project builds confidence so that you can tackle a larger project next!

Hand Quilting

A running stitch is a simple but stylish accent to add to any quilt. Use it in conjunction with machine stitching or for hand-quilting an entire piece.

Quilting by hand used to be the standard. With a hoop and thimble (and a little practice), anyone can do it anywhere. However, it is time consuming and can wreak havoc on your fingers. Lately, it has become popular to use larger stitches and colorful perle cotton to add hand quilting as a decorative accent. It's beautiful on its own or combined with simple machine stitching. It can be a wonderfully slow, meditative way to commune with your special fabrics and consider each one as you stitch through them.

Try alternating straight-line machine quilting with a large running stitch by hand, using a size 8 or 12 perle cotton in a color that accentuates your quilt. This is especially nice on medium-sized projects like pillows, table runners, or throw quilts.

Tying

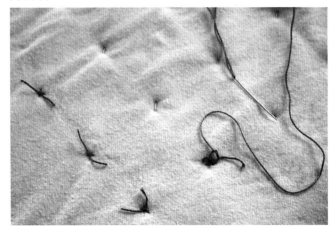

For Mike's Star Quilt (page 115), I didn't want the ends of the ties showing on the front of the quilt. From the front, I marked with pins where I wanted the ties to be (which also did the job of basting the layers), then turned the quilt over and tied from the back, close to the pins.

Tying your quilt is a classic way of holding the layers together. Acrylic yarn tends to untie, but wool yarn, cotton embroidery floss, or perle cotton are great choices. Using a needle with an eye large enough for your yarn or floss, poke through all the layers of your quilt at the desired spot, then come up about ⅛"–¼" (3–6mm) away. Poke back down at the original spot and then back up through the second spot. Tie the yarn or floss ends in a square knot and trim the excess to about 1" (2.5cm).

You can make each tie individually, or you can use a longer length and do all the needlework for multiple ties (leaving long tails in between them), then snip and tie the tails later. Whichever method you use, ties should be placed no more than one hand's width apart from each other. You can tie a throw or bed quilt relatively quickly and easily.

Tying Diagram

Longarm Quilting

My sister-in-law calls this "quilting by check." In many areas, there are people with longarm quilting machines who you can pay to do the quilting for you. Choosing a computer-guided, overall design is usually the most cost-effective, but call around and ask what your options are. There is no basting necessary—you just hand off your quilt top and backing. Typically, providing the batting is optional (often the long armer will supply the batting for a charge). The long-armer returns your piece quilted and ready for binding. Some will even bind for you for an extra fee. Longarm quilting is great for large quilts that you don't want to have to squish through your domestic machine or when you want a more intricate or regular quilting design than you feel comfortable creating on your own.

Binding

I like sewing the binding onto the quilt by machine, then hand-sewing the edge wrapped to the back. However, it's worth checking out variations, such as sewing it all by machine or creating a flanged (or faux-piped) binding. Whichever way you plan on attaching the binding, here are the basic steps.

1. Trim the edges of your quilt even and square. This means cutting off the excess batting and backing, and if necessary, cutting some of your border if the quilt is really out of whack.

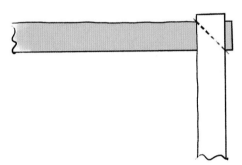

2. Cut 2½" (6.4cm) x WOF strips from your binding fabric. Place ends at a right angle, right sides together, and sew together on the diagonal to make one joined strip. Trim seam allowance to ¼" (6mm). Add strips until the binding is long enough to go around your quilt with at least 18" (45.7cm) extra. Iron the strip in half lengthwise,

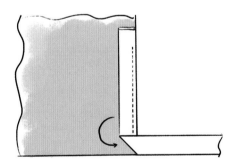

wrong sides together.

3. Sew on the binding, matching raw edges. Leave a tail approximately 9" (22.9cm) long and start in the middle of a side. When you reach a corner, stop ¼" (6mm) from the end and remove the quilt from the machine. Fold the

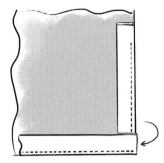

binding back, away from the quilt, forming a diagonal fold in the corner.

4. Fold the binding back. Align raw edges with the next side, and form another fold along the first side. Sew the binding to the next side, beginning at the corner. This will

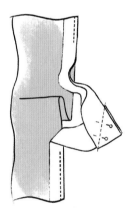

form a neat corner when folded to the back side of the quilt. Sew the rest of the corners in the same way.

5. To join the ends of the binding, stop sewing at least 6" (15.2cm) from where you began. Lay one binding "tail" over the other. Cut the bottom strip at about the halfway point of the unsewn area. Cut the top strip so it overlaps by 2½" (6.4cm). Unfold the bottom strip. Lay its end face up next to the quilt. Unfold the top strip. Lay its cut end face down on top of the bottom strip at a 90-degree angle, matching edges. Sew along the diagonal as shown. If you think of the binding strips as "legs": sew across the "hips," not through the "crotch."

6. Make sure the completed binding strip is the right length, and not twisted. Then trim the excess seam allowance. Sew the unsewn section to the quilt, matching raw edges, as with the rest of the binding.

7. Turn the folded edge of the binding to the back side of the quilt. Sew in place using an appliqué or whipstitch, covering the line of stitching used to attach the binding.

Memory Projects

Because memory quilts and projects are inherently unique, I wanted to bring some of that individuality into this book—to help you imagine how you'd like to tell your story.

This section has patterns for quilts and other items, but also a description of the person that each project was made for. They tell the significance of the fabrics given to me to work with. My hope is that you, the reader, may see a bit of your story in one or more of theirs, and this will help guide you in creating something special with your own sentimental fabrics.

In some cases, I've included a project variation that utilizes a different amount of fabric, since what you have may not be the same as what I had to work with. I've also included a few suggestions for color, fabric, or uses at the beginning of each pattern. Yardage given for an accent or purchased fabrics is based on 44" (111.8cm) wide quilting cottons. The amount of special fabric listed is an approximation based on a men's size-large shirt. You may need more or less, depending on the garments you are working with. Feel free to adjust as desired. This book is all about options and flexibility.

32 Mike's Stars
Mike's Story, 32
Log Star Pillow, 34
Anvil Star Pillow, 37
Sawtooth Star Pillow, 38
Variation: Scrappy Star Quilt, 42

44 Ralph's Square Dance
Ralph's Story, 44
Square Dance Quilt, 46

48 Gregory's Wonky Stars
Gregory's Story, 48
Wonky Star Quilt, 50
Variation: HST Throw Pillow, 54

56 Kenny's Stripes
Kenny's Story, 56
Stripes Quilt, 58

60 Joni's Pathway
Joni's Story, 60
Pathway Table Runner, 62
Variation: Patio Pillow, 66

68 Angela's Aspens
Angela's Story, 68
Aspens Quilt, 70

72 Constanze's Textile Art
Constanze's Story, 72
Flock Wall Art, 74
Hearth Wall Art, 76
Arcs Wall Art, 79
Grow Wall Art, 81
Waterfall Wall Art, 83
Art's Story, 84

86 Art's Portal
Art's Story, 86
Portal Quilt, 88

90 Eden's Cairn
Eden's Story, 90
Cairn Table Runner, 92
Variation: Small Cairn Quilt, 98

100 Katja's Froggy Monster
Katja's Story, 100
Froggy-Monster Backpack, 102
Variation: Just a Stuffie, 107

110 Tanner's Patchwork
Tanner's Story, 110
Patchwork Tote, 112

Mike's Stars

Mike's Story

Mike enlisted in the US Army as a technician to do explosive ordnance disposal—he was a bomb squad guy. He deployed to Kuwait and then Iraq for the first war there, operations Desert Shield and Desert Storm. Mike went on to officer candidate school, after which he was commissioned as an officer in the Military Intelligence Corps. He then transitioned from active duty to the Army Reserves where he continued to have a very active career, deploying to a number of other locations in support of the war effort.

When I asked him if he was willing to be a test for my memory-quilt concept, he jumped right on the opportunity. Mike wanted to use fabric from each of the various, representative uniforms he had saved throughout his career. The patriotic star and its bold look appealed to him, as did the red color scheme. He focused in on the idea that the quilt could represent his years of service:

> *Reflecting on what your quilt means to me, I look at it on a daily basis. If I had to sum up my feelings toward it and what it represents, I think the one word would be "therapeutic." It is one of my most prized possessions.*
>
> *Each uniform swatch and unit patch marks a point in time within a long career of service. Service not to our country, but to the guys on my left and right. Brothers-in-arms that I could not or would never fail. Our country on the whole may not often care, but as brothers we covered each other.*
>
> *As years went by, reflection turns to the soldiers I had the privilege to lead. I reflect on their names, faces, and time spent together (good/bad, peacetime/ war) with fondness. I especially reflect on those no longer with us and the families they've left behind.*

For Mike, his quilt is something he can interact with both physically and psychologically. It is not merely a daily reminder of his years of service, but also something personal and thoughtful. It is soft, like his leadership style. It is another way to remember and mark a career of service in addition to the framed certificates and coins seen in many an officer's memorabilia. It allows him to snuggle under the quilt with his family, and share his history in a tactile, engaging way. The Star pillows in this chapter are inspired by the original quilt I made for Mike (page 115).

Log Star Pillow

DIMENSIONS: 17½" X 17½" (44.5 X 44.5CM)

Shows off three to four special fabrics, but any one of them can be replaced with a coordinating solid if you have fewer special fabrics or want to stretch them to make pillows for multiple friends or family members.

Pillow Backs

In these pillow projects, you can mix and match the pillow tops with pillow back options. If using a shirt with a button or zipper opening, save the front of the shirt for the back of the pillow. There are also instructions for a zipper back if you don't have a shirt to use.

YARDAGE
Special fabric: 4 shirts, or 3 shirts if using background fabric for the Log Cabin center
Background fabric: ½ yard (45.7cm)

CUTTING
From background fabric, cut:
- (4) 5½" x 5½" (14 x 14cm) squares for M
- (4) 4½" x 4½" (11.4 x 11.4cm) squares for N
- (2) 1½" (3.8cm) x WOF strips, subcut into (2) 16½" x 1½" (41.9 x 3.8cm) rectangles and (2) 18½" x 1½" (47 x 3.8cm) rectangles for borders

From special fabric 1, cut:
- (1) 1½" x 2½" (3.8 x 6.4cm) rectangle for A

From special fabric 2, cut:
- (2) 2½" x 2½" (6.4 x 6.4cm) squares for B
- (1) 1½" x 5½" (3.8 x 14cm) rectangle for C
- (1) 2½" x 5½" (6.4 x 14cm) rectangle for D

From special fabric 3, cut:
- (1) 1½" x 5½" (3.8 x 14cm) rectangle for E
- (1) 2½" x 6½" (6.4 x 16.5cm) rectangle for F
- (1) 2½" x 7½" (6.4 x 19.1cm) rectangle for G
- (1) 1½" x 8½" (3.8 x 21.6cm) rectangle for H

From special fabric 4, cut:
- (4) 5½" x 5½" (14 x 14cm) squares for O

Log Cabin

Use ¼" (6mm) seam allowance throughout. Press seams away from the center as you go.

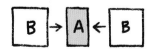

1. First round: Starting with the Log Cabin center (A), sew B pieces on each 2½" (6.4cm) side of the A piece.

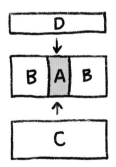

2. Sew C to the bottom long edge of BAB. Sew D to the top following the diagram.

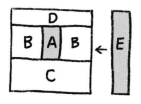

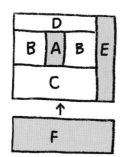

Star Points

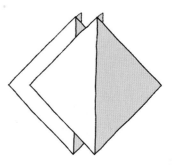

5. Pair each M square, right sides together, with an O square. Following the instructions on page 25, create eight HSTs. Trim each HST block to 4½" x 4½" (11.4 x 11.4cm) if necessary.

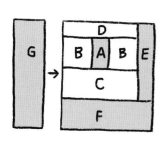

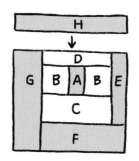

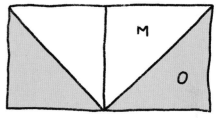

6. Sew two HSTs together along one M side to create one star point unit. This will form a V of background color as shown. Repeat for the remainder of HSTs. Press seam allowances open.

3. **Second round:** Sew piece E to the right side of the first round as in the diagram. Rotate 90 degrees counterclockwise, and sew on piece F. Rotate again and add piece G. Rotate once more and sew piece H to the top of the block.

4. **The completed Log Cabin block should measure 8½" x 8½" (21.6 x 21.6cm).** Trim if necessary.

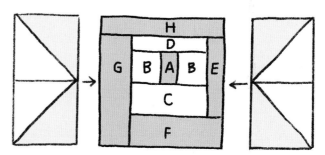

7. Sew one star point unit to each side of the center Log Cabin block as shown. Press seams toward the Log Cabin.

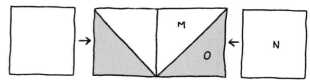

8. Sew the N squares to each end of the two remaining star point units. Press seams toward the squares.

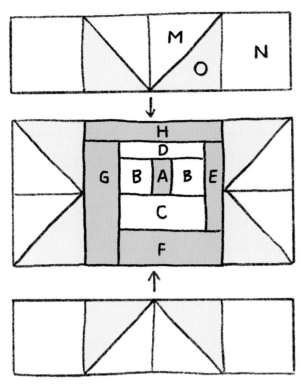

9. Sew the two units from step 8 to the top and bottom of the Log Cabin block to complete the Log Star. The star unit should measure 16½" x 16½" (41.9 x 41.9cm).

Borders

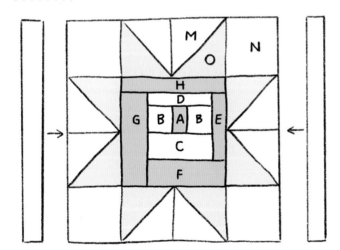

10. Sew the 1½" x 16½" (3.8 x 41.9cm) strips to opposite sides of the Log Star unit. Press strips away from the center.

11. Sew the 1½" x 18½" (3.8 x 47cm) strips to the remaining two sides. Press strips away from the center.

12. Finish with either Pillow Back 1 or 2 (pages 40 and 41).

Anvil Star Pillow

DIMENSIONS: 17½" X 17½" (44.5 X 44.5CM)

A special fabric is the focus as the center (maybe a favorite baby onesie, a pocket, or the embroidery on a logo shirt). The background can be either a special fabric or a coordinating solid.

Star Points

Use ¼" (6mm) seam allowance throughout.

1. Pair each accent square, right sides together, with a 5½" x 5½" (14 x 14cm) special fabric 2 square. Following the instructions on page 25, create eight HSTs. Trim each HST block to 4½" x 4½" (11.4 x 11.4cm) if necessary.

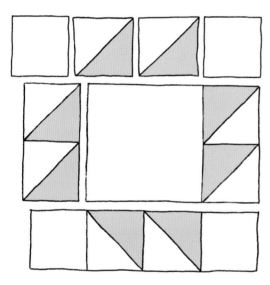

2. Sew HSTs together in pairs according to the diagram. The accent angle is leaning to the same side. You will have four star point units. Press seam allowances open.

3. Sew one star point unit each to the left and right sides of your center block. Pay attention to the direction of the accent triangles—they should angle up on the right side and angle down on the left. Press seams toward the center.

4. Sew a corner square to each end of the two remaining star point units. Press seams toward the squares.

5. Sew these two units to the top and bottom of the center block to complete the Anvil Star. Pay attention to the direction of the accent triangles—they should angle

YARDAGE
Special fabric: 2 shirts
Accent fabric: ¼ yard (22.9cm) or Fat Quarter

CUTTING
From accent fabric, cut:
   (4) 5½" x 5½" (14 x 14cm) squares for star points

From special fabric 1, cut:
   (1) 8½" x 8½" (21.6 x 21.6cm) square for center

From special fabric 2, cut:
   (4) 5½" x 5½" (14 x 14cm) squares for star points

   (4) 4½" x 4½" (11.4 x 11.4cm) squares for corners

   (2) 1½" (3.8cm) x WOF strips, subcut into (2) 16½" x 1½" (41.9 x 3.8cm) rectangles and (2) 18½" x 1½" (47 x 3.8cm) rectangles for borders

right on the top and angle right on the bottom. Press seam allowances toward the center. The star unit should measure 16½" x 16½" (41.9 x 41.9cm).

Borders

6. Sew the 1½" x 16½" (3.8 x 41.9cm) strips to opposite sides of the Anvil Star unit. Press strips away from the center.

7. Sew the 1½" x 18½" (3.8 x 47cm) strips to the remaining two sides. Press strips away from the center.

8. Finish with either Pillow Back 1 or 2 (pages 40 and 41).

Sawtooth Star Pillow

DIMENSIONS: 17½" X 17½" (44.5 X 44.5CM)

This pillow is a great opportunity to use special fabrics as the background and coordinating solids for the star itself. Or flip it and use special fabrics for the star (two similar fabrics for the center will blend nicely) and coordinating solids for the background. Accent fabrics can be replaced with additional special fabrics.

Star Points

Use ¼" (6mm) seam allowance throughout.

1. Pair each 5½" x 5½" (14 x 14cm) accent square, right sides together, with 5½" x 5½" (14 x 14cm) special fabric square. You will have two pairs with special fabric 1 and two pairs with special fabric 2. Following the instructions on page 25, create eight HSTs. Trim each HST block to 4½" x 4½" (11.4 x 11.4cm) if necessary.

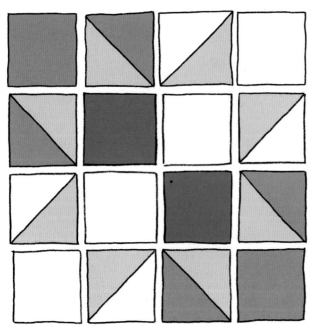

2. Arrange the units according to the diagram. Included are HSTs, 4½" x 4½" (11.4 x 11.4cm) corner squares, and 4½" x 4½" (11.4 x 11.4cm) center squares.

3. Place the second piece in each row right side down over the first piece and chain-stitch the paired pieces together. Place each third piece right side down over each second piece and chain-stitch the pairs together. Place the final pieces and chain-stitch in the same manner. Press seam allowances in each row in opposite directions.

YARDAGE

Special fabric: 2 shirts
Accent fabrics:
Star points and border: ⅓ yard (30.5cm)
Center fabric 1: ¼ yard (22.9cm) or Fat Quarter
Center fabric 2: ¼ yard (22.9cm) or Fat Quarter

CUTTING

From special fabrics, cut (from each):
  (2) 5½" x 5½" (14 x 14cm) squares for star points
  (2) 4½" x 4½" (11.4 x 11.4cm) squares for corners
From accent fabrics, cut:
  (4) 5½" x 5½" (14 x 14cm) squares for star points
  (2) 4½" x 4½" (11.4 x 11.4cm) squares each of two fabrics for star center
  (2) 1½" (3.8cm) x WOF strips, subcut into (2) 16½" x 1½" (41.9 x 3.8cm) rectangles and (2) 18½" x 1½" (47 x 3.8cm) rectangles for borders

4. Pin the rows together, nesting the seam allowances. Sew to complete the Sawtooth Star. Press seam allowances either open or to one side. The star unit should measure 16½" x 16½" (41.9 x 41.9cm).

Borders

5. Sew the 1½" x 16½" (3.8 x 41.9cm) strips to opposite sides of the star unit. Press strips away from the center.

6. Sew the 1½" x 18½" (3.8 x 47cm) strips to the remaining two sides. Press strips away from the center.

7. Finish with either Pillow Back 1 or 2 (pages 40 and 41).

Any one of these pillows make for a special project, but you can also make a whole collection of stars.

Pillow Back 1

Assembly

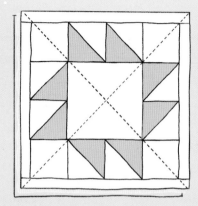

YARDAGE AND SUPPLIES

Batting: 20" x 20" (50.8 x 50.8cm)

Lining: 20" x 20" (50.8 x 50.8cm), or ⅝ yard (57.2cm) muslin or scrap fabric

Special fabric: 1 shirt front with button opening or nonmetal zipper

Binding: ¼ yard (22.9cm)

18" (45.7cm) pillow form

1. Sandwich the block with batting and lining at least 1" (2.5cm) **larger all around.** Quilt as desired. Trim excess batting and lining. Your quilted pillow front should be 18½" x 18½" (47 x 47cm) or close to it. Sew on any buttons or patches.

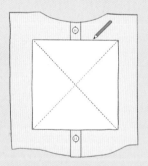
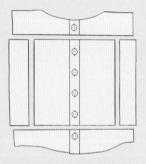

2. Lay your pillow front on top of the shirt front in the desired position and trace around it. Cut along the traced line. If you are using a top with a zipper front, make sure that the zipper tab is pulled down within the area that will be the pillow back. Cut through any excess zipper with scissors, not your rotary cutter.

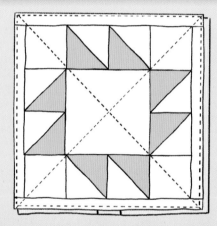

3. Place the pillow back, right side down, on your work surface. Place the quilted pillow front on top, wrong sides together. Pin in place. Baste around all four sides using the longest stitch length your machine allows. If you have a plastic zipper to sew through, go slowly as some sewing machines won't have the power to go through. Use a size 90/14 or 100/16 topstitch needle to go through all the layers more easily.

4. Bind the pillow as if binding a quilt (page 29). As with basting, go slowly through the zipper if your back has one. Insert an 18" (45.7cm) pillow form through the button or zipper opening and enjoy!

Pillow Back 2

YARDAGE AND SUPPLIES

Batting: 20" x 20" (50.8 x 50.8cm)

Lining: 20" x 20" (50.8 x 50.8cm), or ⅝ yard (57.2cm) muslin or scrap fabric

Back and binding: ¾ yard (68.6cm) coordinating fabric

20" (50.8cm) or longer zipper

18" (45.7cm) pillow form

CUTTING

From backing fabric, cut:

(1) 18½" x 7¾" (47 x 19.7cm) rectangle

(1) 18½" x 13" (47 x 33cm) rectangle

Assembly

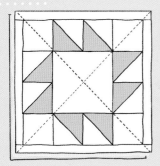

1. Sandwich the block with batting and lining at least 1" (2.5cm) larger all around. Quilt as desired. Trim excess batting and lining. Your pillow form should be 18½" x 18½" (47 x 47cm) or close to it. Sew on any buttons or patches.

2. On one 18½" (47cm) side of each backing rectangle, serge or zigzag the edge to finish. On the smaller rectangle, fold over 1" (2.5cm) from the serged edge and press.

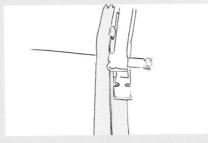

3. Lay the larger rectangle right side up. Place the zipper right side down along the serged edge. The zipper will be longer than the fabric, so the ends will extend beyond the fabric and the zipper pull will be out of the way while sewing. Using a zipper foot, stitch approximately ¼" (6mm) from the edge of the zipper.

4. Turn the fabric and zipper over. Press the fabric away from the zipper. Topstitch the fabric close to the fold.

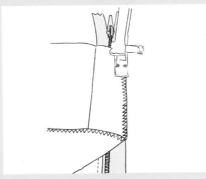

5. Unfold the pressed edge of the smaller fabric rectangle. Place the serged edge on top of the remaining edge of the zipper, right sides together. Be sure the fabric rectangle lines up with the already sewn rectangle. Sew approximately ¼" (6mm) from the zipper and serged fabric edge.

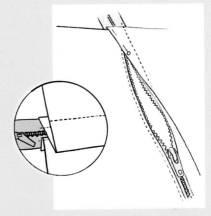

6. Fold the fabric along the pressed line to create the flap that covers the zipper. Pin in place. From the back side, sew between the last line of stitching and the edge of the zipper to stitch the flap in place. Open the zipper a few inches and pin the flap down near the open end of the zipper. This will keep everything in the correct place when sewing the pillow back to the pillow front.

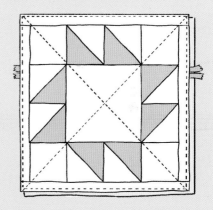

7. Place the pillow back on your work surface, right side down. Place the quilted pillow front block on top of it, wrong sides together. Trim pillow back to size if necessary. Pin in place and baste around all four sides. Trim off the excess zipper length.

8. Bind the pillow as if binding a quilt (page 29). Insert an 18" (45.7cm) pillow form through the zipper opening and enjoy!

YARDAGE

Star Center (Hearth): ⅛ yard (11.4cm), or special fabric scrap
Log Cabin round 1: 1 shirt front or arms, or ¼ yard (22.9cm)
Log Cabin round 2: 1 shirt front or arms, or ¼ yard (22.9cm)
Log Cabin round 3: 1 shirt, or ⅜ yard (34.3cm)
Star Points: 1 shirt back, or ⅔ yard (61cm)
Background fabric: 3 or more shirts, or 2 yards (1.8m)
Backing: 3 yards (2.7m)
Binding: ½ yard (45.7cm)
Batting: 52" x 58" (1.3 x 1.5m)

CUTTING

From background fabric, cut:
  (76) 6½" x 6½" (16.5 x 16.5cm) squares for the background and N

  (4) 7¼" x 7¼" (18.4 x 18.4cm) squares for M

From Star Points, cut:
  (4) 7¼" x 7¼" (18.4 x 18.4cm) squares for O

From Star Center, cut:
  (1) 1½" x 2½" (3.8 x 6.4cm) rectangle for A

From Log Cabin round 1, cut:
  (2) 2½" x 2½" (6.4 x 6.4cm) squares for B
  (1) 1½" x 5½" (3.8 x 14cm) rectangle for C
  (1) 2½" x 5½" (6.4 x 14cm) rectangle for D

From Log Cabin round 2, cut:
  (1) 1½" x 5½" (3.8 x 14cm) rectangle for E
  (1) 2½" x 6½" (6.4 x 16.5cm) rectangle for F
  (1) 2½" x 7½" (6.4 x 19.1cm) rectangle for G
  (1) 1½" x 8½" (3.8 x 21.6cm) rectangle for H

From Log Cabin round 3, cut:
  (1) 2" x 8½" (5.1 x 21.6cm) rectangle for I
  (1) 3" x 10" (7.6 x 25.4cm) rectangle for J
  (1) 3" x 11" (7.6 x 27.9cm) rectangle for K
  (1) 2" x 12½" (5.1 x 31.8cm) rectangle for L

Variation:

Scrappy Star Quilt

DIMENSIONS: 48" X 54" (1.2 X 1.4M)

This pattern will create a lap quilt with a single bold star and a scrappy background. This is a great pattern for when you have lots of similarly colored and subtly patterned shirts. The star can be a combination of contrasting special fabrics or solid accent fabrics—your choice.

Log Cabin

Use ¼" (6mm) seam allowance throughout. Press seams away from the center as you go.

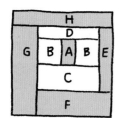

1. Follow steps 1–3 of Log Star Pillow Top (pages 34 and 35). The Log Cabin block used in this quilt is the same as the Log Star Pillow center and first two rounds.

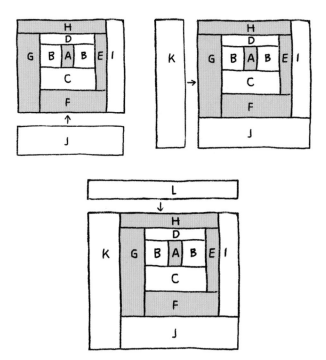

2. Third round: Sew piece I to the right side of the second round as in the diagram. Rotate 90 degrees counterclockwise, and sew on piece J. Rotate again and add piece K. Rotate once more and sew piece L to the top of the block.

3. The completed Log Cabin block should measure 12½" x 12½" (31.8 x 31.8cm). Trim if necessary.

Star Points

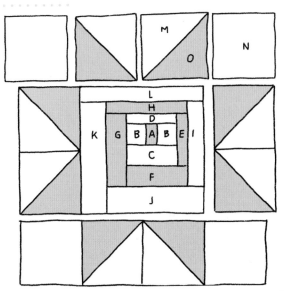

4. Follow steps 5–9 of Log Star Pillow Top but trim the HSTs to 6½" x 6½" (16.5 x 16.5cm). Sew units together according to the diagram. The star unit should measure 24½" x 24½" (62.2 x 62.2cm).

Assembly

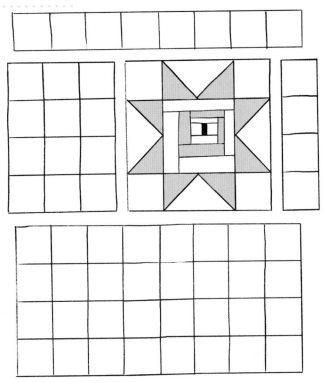

5. Arrange the 72 remaining 6½" x 6½" (16.5 x 16.5cm) background squares. Sew together into background sections as follows, distributing the various special fabrics evenly throughout. Press to nest seams where appropriate.

- Top row: 8 squares across (48½" x 6½" [123.2 x 16.5cm])

- Left of the Star block: 3 squares across x 4 squares tall (18½" x 24½" [47 x 62.2cm])

- Right of the Star block: 4 squares tall (6½" x 24½" [16.5 x 62.2cm])

- Bottom section: 8 squares across x 4 squares tall (48½" x 24½" [123.3 x 62.2cm])

6. Sew the sections to the Star block according to the diagram. Work in this order: left of star section, right of star section, top row, and bottom section.

7. Sew patches, nametapes, etc., back on as a final touch. Pay attention to placement. Your quilt top is complete. Layer the quilt top, batting, and backing. Quilt and bind as desired.

Ralph's Square Dance

Ralph's Story

Ralph is a tenured fire service employee who has been with the Prescott Fire Department for 29 years. He holds the rank of chief of operations, overseeing all firefighters and stations in the department. He is also an operations chief for the US Forest Service during the summer and travels to fight wildland fires all over the US as part of Southwest Incident Management Team 1. Ralph and his wife, Jen, have been married for 27 years and have three daughters. They are a busy, active family that does a lot together. Ralph describes himself as motivated and passionate about true leadership and treats everyday as if it is a gift.

When I asked Ralph, through my sister whose family is friends with his, if I could make a memory quilt for him, he thought it was incredible that someone would reach out and do something like this. He knows the quilt will memorialize his career and will be something that he will cherish and reflect upon.

The T-shirts Ralph sent me come from many of his firefighter-related travels and experiences. He was able to go to New York City following September 11th and support the New York City Fire Department with a group of other firefighters, so some shirts are from that period. Other shirts are simply duty shirts that he wanted to memorialize in the quilt. Ralph was honor guard commander for the department, so there is a shirt for that. He was also a part of a tragedy that occurred within his own fire department where 19 firefighters were killed at the Yarnell Hill Fire in 2013. He included many shirts commemorating that wildland fire, which became a defining point in his life.

When I asked Ralph what he will do with the quilt, he responded, "I will use it! I will also take really good care of it and share it with my family and grandkids. It will be passed through our family for hopefully a very long time. It will become a family heirloom."

Proof positive that a quilt made from meaningful fabrics tells as much of a story as words do.

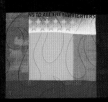
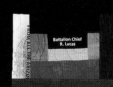

Square Dance Quilt

DIMENSIONS: 60" X 72" (1.5 X 1.8M)

This quilt design is perfect for when you have T-shirts with large designs you'd rather not cut up, like Ralph's, or for those Hawaiian shirts with great patterns! This quilt alternates "plain" 12" (30.5cm) blocks with improvisationally pieced Log Cabin blocks. Improvisation is created in the moment, so in this quilt, it means that there is no specific measurement for the "logs" in the pieced blocks. Each Log Cabin block is constructed from the center square out and then trimmed to the desired size, making them great for utilizing smaller design elements on a shirt for the centers or for the logs themselves—just cut the size that works for your special fabric.

Choose seven colors for your uneven Log Cabins that pick up on the colors in your special fabrics. I chose the fiery yellows to reds already in Ralph's T-shirts and added cool blues and purple to signify water. For a project like a graduation-themed T-shirt quilt, consider school colors and add a lighter and darker version of each. You will also use scraps of the special fabrics within the Log Cabins to create rhythm and movement across the quilt, blurring the lines between the solid blocks and the Log Cabin blocks.

To visualize the final block, it is helpful when trimming to use a large 12½" (31.8cm) square ruler or a larger ruler with the 12½" (31.8cm) lines marked with blue painter's tape or washi tape. Use ¼" (6mm) seam allowance throughout. Press all seams from the back to protect the T-shirt motifs.

Log Cabin Blocks

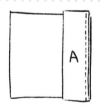

1. Choose a center square (accent fabric or special fabric). Cut a piece of fabric A slightly longer than the center square and place it, right sides together, on the right edge of the center square. Sew the strip in place. Press the strip away from the center.

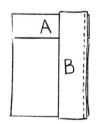

2. Turn the block counterclockwise. The previous strip will be at the top. Add a strip of fabric B to the right edge, confirming it's cut long enough to cover the center square plus the previously sewn strip. Sew the strip in place. Press the strip away from the center. Trim any excess seam allowance from the first strip.

YARDAGE

Special fabric: 15 T-shirts, or enough special fabric to cut (15) 12½" x 12½" (31.8 x 31.8cm) squares

Accent fabrics:

Log Cabin centers: ¼ yard (22.9cm)

Log Cabin color group 1 (light or warm) sides: ⅜ yard (34.3cm) each of 3 fabrics (A, B, E, and F)

Log Cabin color group 2 (dark or cool) sides: ⅜ yard (34.3cm) each of 3 fabrics (C, D, G, and H)

Backing: 3¾ yards (3.4m)
Binding: ½ yard (45.7cm)
Batting: 64" x 76" (1.6 x 1.9m)

CUTTING

From special fabric, cut:

(15) 12½" x 12½" (31.8 x 31.8cm) squares, one from each T-shirt or as many as necessary from clothing with an overall print.

(1) 2"–3" (5.1–7.6cm) wide strip from each T-shirt, or at least one strip from each special fabric that you used for the large squares.

Small motifs from T-shirts for Log Cabin centers. They can be any size, up to about 6" x 6" (15.2 x 15.2cm) for best results. You can use these for some, or all, of the centers.

From accent fabrics, cut:

Optional: 4½" x 4½" (11.4 x 11.4cm) squares for Log Cabin centers. You can use these for some, or all, of the centers.

(2) 2"–3" (5.1–7.6cm) wide strips from each remaining accent fabric. You may need to cut more as you sew.

3. Turn the block and add a strip of fabric C to the right edge. Check the length. This is also a color change: the first two strips are from one color group (light or warm); this and the next strip will be from your other color group (dark or cool). Sew the strip in place. Press the strip away from the center. Trim any excess seam allowance from the second strip.

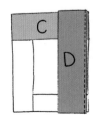

4. Turn the block and add a strip of fabric D to the right edge. Check the length. Sew the strip in place. Press the strip away from the center. Trim any excess seam allowance from the third strip.

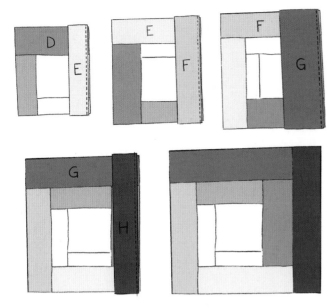

Assembly

5. Continue adding strips in this manner around all four sides of the block. Keep the color group 1 fabrics on the same two sides of the block and the color group 2 fabrics on the other two. Add fabrics E and F, then G and H (or special fabric), until your block is at least 12½" x 12½" (31.8 x 31.8cm). Feel free to use the same color twice before moving to the next, or start with C and D fabrics and then add the A and B fabrics.

6. Add another strip or more if necessary. If doing this, you may want to first trim your block a bit so that your final round of strips will be at least ½" (1.3cm) wide after everything is trimmed to 12½" x 12½" (31.8 x 31.8cm). At least one of the strips in the last round should be special fabric.

7. Trim the block to 12½" x 12½" (31.8 x 31.8cm) using your rotary cutter and ruler. Repeat steps 1–6 for each center square fabric piece for a total of 15 Log Cabin blocks.

8. Arrange the blocks. Alternate 12½" x 12½" (31.8 x 31.8cm) "plain" blocks with pieced Log Cabin blocks as in the diagram. If you match the special fabric strips in the Log Cabin blocks with a plain block of the same fabric, the eye will blend them and break up the strict grid of the quilt, creating a more dynamic composition.

9. Sew the rows together. Press seam allowances toward the plain blocks.

10. Sew columns together. Nest the seams at the block intersections.

11. Sew patches, nametapes, etc., back on as a final touch. Pay attention to placement. Your quilt top is complete. Layer the quilt top, batting, and backing. Quilt and bind as desired.

Because I'm using a lot of bright colors here, I arranged the strips so the cool colors are kept to one corner and the warm colors to the other. This helps to make the block look intentional.

Gregory's Wonky Stars

Gregory's Story

Gregory has been a lifelong theater maker, artist, and teacher. He currently lives in Portland, Oregon, and is the theater program director at the University of Portland where he teaches design, choreography, and musical theater.

Gregory's father, Don, grew up in Wisconsin and always admired Pendleton wool shirts. In the '30s and '40s, they were a status symbol of someone who loved the outdoors. Don grew up very poor in the Northwoods of Wisconsin, where he hunted and fished for food for his mother, father, and three siblings. He never could afford a Pendleton as a kid. When he was discharged from the army in 1947, he bought his first one. It was a blue plaid. He spoke about it throughout his whole life. He had made it to a status that he had only dreamed about.

Don met Helen at the paper mill in Rhinelander as a bet from his male coworkers. They said, "Let's see how long it will take for Don to ask the new girl out on a date?" It was only two days. Helen and Don began dating and were married two years later in 1950. For their honeymoon, they bought matching Pendleton shirt jackets. Gregory has fond memories (and *so* many adorable pictures) of his parents in those shirts throughout their lives. He remembers the shirts hanging in the hall closet in their house in California when he was a kid and thought, "Why are these scratchy old shirts here?" They were impractical in the California weather but were always brought along on camping trips and cross-country road trips back to Wisconsin.

When Gregory started teaching at Western Washington University in 1999, there was a Pendleton outlet store about 20 miles from his house. It was his first "real" job, so he bought a beautiful wool shirt as a reward for his success. It was a blue plaid. And then he bought another

and another and another. He was just as passionate about the status, look, and comfort of this brand as his father was so many years ago. Living in Bellingham, Washington, Gregory had many occasions to wear them throughout the year and seasons. At the time, Don and Helen lived in Palm Springs, California, and sadly had no use for a wool shirt, but Don admired his son's collection and "borrowed" one whenever he came to visit.

After Helen passed in 2012, Don moved to live close to Gregory and his husband. Don had always wanted a "Christmas" red Pendleton to wear during the holidays . . . and that's exactly what he got that first Christmas in Portland, Oregon. And then another one and another one and a few of Gregory's—all in different shades of reds, maroons, greens, and grays: his favorite colors.

When Don died at age 93 in 2020, Gregory knew that he needed to keep these shirts as a memory of his father, his life, and his legacy. Those shirts stayed packed in a box for two years until, one day, a chance to reimagine them came along.

When the opportunity came to have these shirts made into a quilt, I was thrilled to give Don's collection to the project. Having his shirts continue to warm and comfort me is an amazing feeling and wonderful tribute to his life as a father, explorer, adventurer, and great man. He will be with me now always.

I am so touched and overwhelmed by Kristin's talent and generosity. Don admired her artwork and hospitality and would be touched by such a gift of time and care.

Wonky Star Quilt

ORIGINAL DIMENSIONS: 95" X 95" (2.4 X 2.4M)

TWIN DIMENSIONS: 75" X 85½" (1.9 X 2.2M)

LAP DIMENSIONS: 54" X 64½" (1.4 X 1.6M)

Wonky Stars not only remove the stress of sewing perfect points, but add a wonderful energy to this classic design. Baby onesies might only yield one or two stars per garment while a large men's shirt yields about 15. Don's shirts were a warm collection of wools, but this quilt would be appropriate for just about anything: conservative dress shirts and a navy or bright background color, wildly patterned shirts combined with a favorite solid color, or even baby clothes and a soft coordinating color (and maybe flannel background fabric). The large amount of background fabric does a great job of unifying the stars, even if they are much more varied than Don's.

Note: This pattern is for a Queen- to King-sized quilt, but you can easily make it smaller by reducing the number of rows and columns. Changes for the Twin and Lap sizes are in brackets.

YARDAGE

	King	Twin	Lap
Special fabric	5 shirts		
Coordinating fabric	6 yards (5.5m)	4 yards (3.7m)	2 yards (1.8m)
Outer border	1⅛ yards (1m)	1 yard (91.4cm)	⅞ yard (80cm)
Backing	9 yards (8.2m)	5½ yards (5m)	3½ yards (3.2m)
Binding	¾ yard (68.6cm)	⅔ yard (61cm)	½ yard (45.7cm)
Batting	99" x 99" (2.5 x 2.5m)	79" x 90" (2 x 2.3m)	58" x 69" (1.5 x 1.8m)

CUTTING

From background fabric, cut:

> (52 [34, 16]) 4" (10.2cm) x WOF strips, subcut into (512 [336, 160]) 4" x 4" (10.2 x 10.2cm) squares for background

> (9 [8, 7]) 4" (10.2cm) x WOF strips for outer border

From special fabric, cut:

> (64 [42, 20]) 4" x 4" (10.2 x 10.2cm) squares for star centers. Divide the number of squares by the number of like-sized garments you are using to determine how many center squares to cut from each special fabric (e.g., 13 each from five different shirts for King size).

> (3–4) 2" (5.1cm) strips from the longest section of your garments for inner border—enough to add up to about 352" [276", 192"] (8.9m [7m, 4.9m])

> (3–4) 2" x 2" (5.1 x 5.1cm) squares of each fabric

> (256 [168, 80]) 4" x 4" (10.2 x 10.2cm) squares, subcut in half diagonally for star points (a little larger is better if you have a hard time making your points)

NOTES ON FUSSY CUTTING

One of my pattern testers, Brittany, dug into her large collection of scraps to test this pattern. Many of her quilting cottons had wonderful designs that she highlighted by "fussy cutting" so that the desired design was in the middle of her 4" x 4" (10.2 x 10.2cm) Wonky Star center squares. We both thought that this could also be a great opportunity to show off small T-shirt logos and embroidered emblems. I like to take blue painter's tape and place it on my rotary ruler 4" (10.2cm) to the side, and down, from one corner to make a quick "window" to place over the design to check placement as you cut. I also use this technique when rough-cutting (page 14). Remember to consider that your stitching will be ¼" (6mm) inside the tape and ruler edges.

Star Points

1. Match eight triangles or scraps to make the star points. Pick four background squares, which will be the base for the star points. The points will be sewn using the stitch-and-flip method.

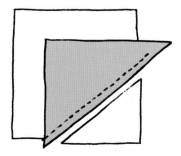

2. Place a triangle, right side up, in the lower-right corner of the square where you want a star point. Flip on the long edge so it is wrong side down on the background. Scoot it about ¼" (6mm) toward the corner. Sew ¼" (6mm) from the edge of the flipped fabric. Before trimming anything, make sure that the star point extends to or beyond the lower-right corner of the background square. Restitch if necessary to cover the corner.

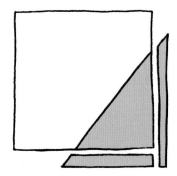

3. Trim the excess background and special fabric under the star point, leaving a ¼" (6mm) seam allowance. Press along the seam line so the triangle is face up again. Trim the block so it is 4" x 4" (10.2 x 10.2cm).

4. Repeat steps 2–3 for the remaining three background/ star point pairs in this set. Each background square should now have one star point. I like to work in sets because some of the trimmings from the first round of star points may be used to make the second round, thus conserving fabric.

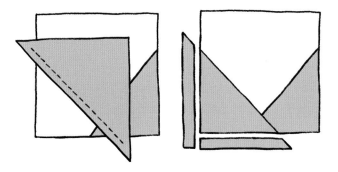

5. Repeat steps 2–4 but placing the star point in the opposite, lower corner. Now each background square will have two star points.

6. Repeat steps 1–5 for the rest of the stars. Make 256 [168, 80] star points that coordinate with your 64 [42, 20] star centers.

Wonky Stars

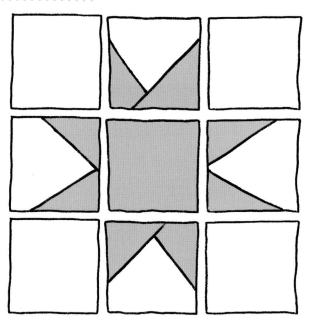

7. Arrange the units according to the diagram. Included are four background corner squares, four matching star points, and one star center.

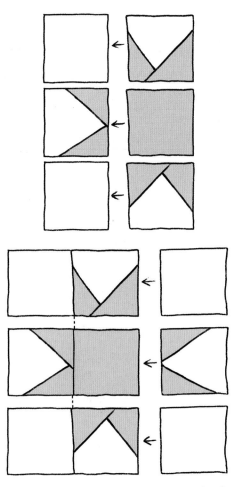

8. Chain-piece (page 24) all star sets. Sew the first two pieces in each row together in a chain, continuing to the next two sets and so on. Add the third piece in each row, creating a "web" three squares wide by 64 [42, 20] squares long. Cut apart between sets. You should have 64 [42, 20] sets of nine squares held together by a small chain of stitches. Press the seam allowances open for less bulk.

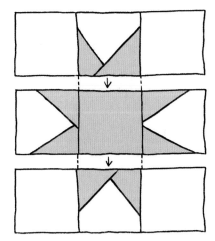

9. Sew the rows in each set, matching the seams. Press the seam allowances open for less bulk. If necessary, trim each Wonky Star block to 10½" x 10½" (26.7 x 26.7cm).

Assembly

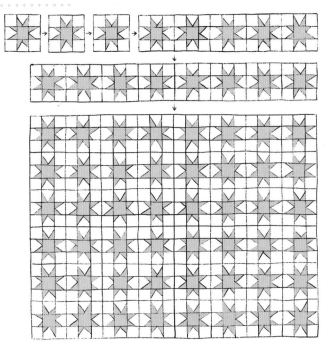

10. Arrange the Wonky Star blocks in 8 rows x 8 blocks [6x7, 4x5]. Chain-piece in columns, sewing the first two star blocks in each row, adding the third block from each row, adding the fourth, etc. This will create a "web" of blocks held together by a small chain of stitches. Press each row in the opposite direction.

11. Sew the rows together. Nest the seams between blocks and match the seams pressed open. Press the seam allowances open to distribute bulk, or press in one direction—whichever your fabrics want to do.

12. Sew the inner-border pieces end to end. Alternate strips and 2" x 2" (5.1 x 5.1cm) squares, mixing up the colors as desired.

13. From the pieced strip, cut two border strips the same length measurement of your quilt. Cut two more the width measurement plus 3¾" (9.5cm). Mark the center of each strip with a pin.

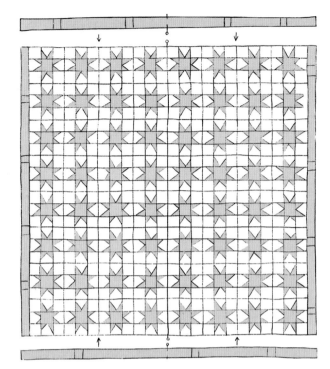

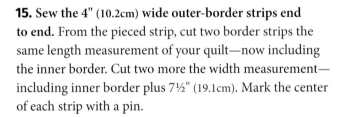

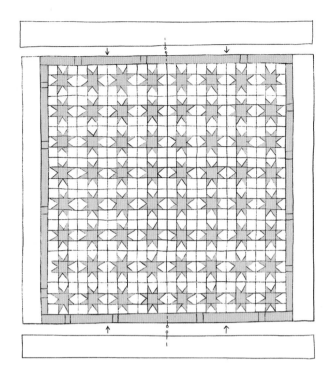

14. Pin the two length inner-border pieces to the left and right sides of the quilt. Match center points and ends. Sew. Press seams toward the borders. Pin, then sew, the two width border pieces to the top and bottom of the quilt, matching center points. Press toward the border.

15. Sew the 4" (10.2cm) wide outer-border strips end to end. From the pieced strip, cut two border strips the same length measurement of your quilt—now including the inner border. Cut two more the width measurement—including inner border plus 7½" (19.1cm). Mark the center of each strip with a pin.

16. Pin the two length outer-border pieces to the left and right sides of the quilt. Match center points and ends. Sew. Press seams toward the borders. Pin, then sew, the two width pieces to the top and bottom of the quilt, matching center points. Press toward the border.

17. Your quilt top is complete. Layer the quilt top, batting, and backing. Quilt and bind as desired. Sew patches, nametapes, etc., back on as a final touch. Pay attention to placement.

Border Measurements

To find the length of the side borders, measure the quilt from top to bottom at the center and each side. Add these measurements together and divide by three for the average; in this quilt, it should be close to 84½" [63", 42"] (2.1m [1.6m, 1.1m]). This is your length.

For the width of your quilt, measure across the top, the center, and the bottom. Calculate the average. In this quilt, it should be close to 84½" [73½", 52½"] (2.1m [1.9m, 1.3m]). This is your width.

YARDAGE AND SUPPLIES
Special fabric: 1–2 shirts, or a variety of scraps
Accent fabric: ¼ yard (22.9cm)
Backing: front of one shirt, or ½ yard (45.7cm)
Binding: ¼ yard (22.9cm)
Batting: 20" x 20" (50.8 x 50.8cm)
18" (45.7cm) zipper in a matching color to the main fabric

CUTTING
From accent fabric, cut:
  (2) 4" (10.2cm) x WOF strips, subcut into (18) 4" x 4" (10.2 x 10.2cm) squares

From special fabric, cut:
  (18) 4" x 4" (10.2 x 10.2cm) squares

Variation:
HST Throw Pillow

If you have leftovers from your Wonky Stars Quilt, you can make a coordinating pillow. Or if you have a variety of special fabrics but don't need as big a project as a whole quilt, this pillow is a great option. For example, Hawaiian shirts paired with a bright solid, or a collection of ties paired with a solid silk or taffeta, make a colorful accent in any room!

Assembly

1. Pair each accent square, right sides together, with a special fabric square. Following the instructions on page 25, create 36 HSTs. Trim each HST block to 3½" x 3½" (8.9 x 8.9cm) if necessary.

2. Arrange all the HST units in six rows of six. Ensure all the triangles are oriented in the same direction.

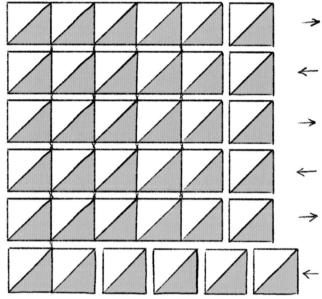

3. Chain-piece in columns, using a ¼" (6mm) seam allowance. Add HST blocks from the top of the pillow to the bottom. Sew the first two blocks in each row, add the third block from each row, the fourth, etc. Press seam allowances in one direction on the first row and the opposite direction on the second row. Alternate pressing directions for the rest of the rows.

4. Sew the rows together to finish piecing the pillow top. Nest the seams. Press seams open.

5. Finish with either Pillow Back 1 or 2 (pages 40 and 41).

Kenny's Stripes

Kenny's Story

My dad, Kenny, has lived in Southern California all his life. After high school, he became a graphic designer, working for several great design offices involved in corporate communications (in his words, rather serious corporate-America stuff). But that wasn't who Kenny really was or wanted to be. In high school, he got bit by the American hot rod and custom-car bug. Obsessed, actually. Eventually, 35 years of corporate communication was enough, and he retired to pursue the classic-car obsession that shaped him for the next 30 years.

Recently, Kenny was cleaning out a closet and discovered two boxes of his old T-shirts. The very next day, I called and told him I had started writing a book on "quilts with a story." In my dad's words, "'Serendipity' is what she called it. I called it a 'very, very special moment.'"

Kenny was open to me creating a quilt or anything with his shirts because, as he says, he's obsessed with car culture—and anything car culture is fun to have around. His home is decorated in a style that he and I refer to as "garage ghastly" (certainly *not* "shabby chic"). The clothes my dad sent were some of his old T-shirts and Levi's® that he wore and worked in through many years. They are the images of the cars he has owned or built, the suppliers and products he used, and the car shows and events that fill his life, as he says:

> *This quilt is the story of my life, who I am, and shows how much my daughter loves me.*
>
> *When the package arrived and I saw what she had created, I was floored. How could I not be? The design, all that labor (and love), the quilting itself, the colors . . . WOW, I shed a tear. No matter how my day has gone, when I enter my living room or bedroom, I can't stop smiling. This all means so much to me.*

In addition to this Stripes throw quilt, I sent a star quilt and several pillows, one of which included a piece of a shirt that my mom had embroidered for him (many years ago, predivorce) of a "pie in the sky." Kind of like Kenny's way of looking at life in general. He found it very fitting and meaningful.

Stripes Quilt

DIMENSIONS: 62" X 74" (1.6 X 1.9M)

This pattern will create a dynamic quilt with random stripes. It is constructed from two ends: the upper-left corner toward the center, and the lower-right corner toward the center. The two sections are sewn together at the end. Depending on the amount of special fabric, and what it is, you can make the quilt smaller or larger, and you can make lots of stripes with your special fabric or use mostly solids with just an accent of special fabric.

The following are some potential options:

1. **Special fabric from one source, plus three near solids.** Example: One fabulous, patterned shirt or dress and three near-solid fabrics in coordinating colors.

2. **Special fabric from several sources.** Example: T-shirts and blue jeans, plus two coordinating near solids.

3. **All special fabric.** Example: Dress shirts in several colors.

This design is more of a formula than a specific pattern. With a general plan in mind for what you will need from each piece of clothing, you are ready to cut. The instructions below assume you have chosen and prepped your special fabric. Special fabric amounts listed below are rough approximations based on a men's size-large shirt, using the back, front, sides, and sleeves.

YARDAGE

Special fabric stripes 1: 3 pairs of blue jeans
Special fabric stripes 2: 3–4 shirts
Coordinating fabric 1: 1 yard (91.4cm)
Coordinating fabric 2: 1 yard (91.4cm)
Backing: 4 yards (3.7m)
Binding: ½ yard (45.7cm)

CUTTING

From coordinating fabric 1, cut:
   (1) 7" x 12" (17.8 x 30.5cm) rectangle for setting corners

From coordinating fabric 2, cut:
   (3) 3" (7.6cm) x WOF strips, subcut into (2) 3" x 42" (7.6 x 106.7cm) strips and (1) 3" x 12" (7.6 x 30.5cm) strip for center stripe

From coordinating fabrics, cut:
   3" (7.6cm) x WOF strips*
   4½" (11.4cm) x WOF strips*
   6½" (16.5cm) x WOF strips*

From special fabrics, cut:
   3" (7.6cm) x WOF strips*
   4½" (11.4cm) x WOF strips*
   6½" (16.5cm) x WOF strips*

* The stripes are cut straight of grain. How many strips you cut of which size depends on your special fabrics. For this quilt, I started by cutting a strip of each width from all my fabrics, then added more as needed when laying out the quilt on my design wall (a floor works well too). It is best to cut as you go.

Straight Stripes

While the stripes are cut straight of grain (following the direction of the threads in the fabric), the ends of the stripes will eventually be cut on an angle. This will create a bias edge that is prone to stretching, which can make your quilt edges wobbly. Consider these notes on taming long strips and bias edges to keep the wobbliness at a minimum:

• Stabilize stretchy fabrics like T-shirts.

• Starching all your fabrics can be helpful.

• Be cognizant of not stretching your strips as you add them. Pinning strips in place while flat will help maintain their length when you sew. If one side of a strip is stretched more than the other, your quilt will not lie flat.

• Don't stress too much—mild "bubbles" can be quilted out.

• Check your progress often.

• Use a stabilizing tape on all the edges when you square up the quilt at the end (see step 9).

Assembly

I used a ⅜" (1cm) seam allowance so that I could sew the jeans strips with the seam allowances on the front where they will fray and give a fun texture to the quilt. If all your seam allowances will be on the back side, then a ¼" (6mm) seam allowance is appropriate.

1. Create the corner setting triangles. Place the 7" x 12" (17.8 x 30.5cm) rectangle on your cutting mat with the 12" (30.5cm) sides vertical. Cut the rectangle diagonally from the lower-left corner to the upper-right corner. This determines the direction all your stripes will go.

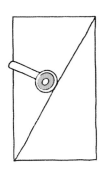

2. Sew the three center-stripe strips end to end. This creates a strip about 94" (2.4m) long. This will be your center strip, though it may not end up exactly in the center.

3. Lay out the strips. Build from the upper-left setting triangle toward the center strip, and from the lower-right setting triangle toward the center strip. Play with placement until you are happy with the result. You will need to sew several strips of fabric end to end to create the needed lengths. Have fun with this! Even once you start sewing the strips together, you can add or subtract strips as you go.

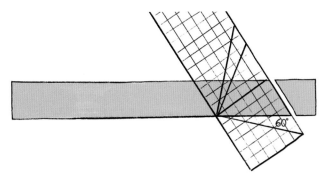

4. Choose the first strip to sew to the upper-left setting triangle. Use the 60-degree line on your ruler to trim the right end of the strip at a 60-degree angle (see diagram). Lay the strip, right side up, next to the corner triangle. Confirm that there is sufficient length for the width of the strip to reach the left side of the quilt. Do not trim the left end yet.

5. Pin the strip to the setting triangle with right sides together. If you want an exposed seam, pin wrong sides together. Align the 60-degree end of the strip to the short side of the setting triangle as in the diagram. Sew the pieces together. Press seam to one side.

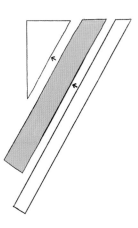

6. Mark the 30-degree angle on the untrimmed end of your strip. Line it up with the long side of the setting triangle. This indicates the left edge of your quilt as you add strips. Be careful to keep the longer (left) edge perpendicular to the shorter (top) edge.

7. Continue to add strips in this manner. Stop when the long, vertical left side measures approximately 74" (1.8m). Add the center strip and set aside.

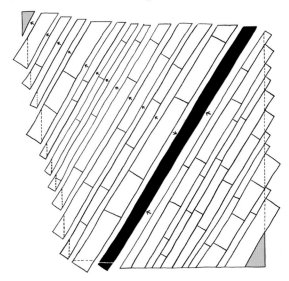

8. Repeat steps 4–7 using the lower-left setting triangle. When both halves are the desired length, decide if the quilt top is wide enough. Add more strips if necessary. Sew the halves together.

9. Trim the edges of your sewn quilt top. Adjust the marked strip ends if necessary. Now is a good time to measure your sides and add stabilizing tape along all four edges to keep the shape during quilting and binding.

10. Sew patches, nametapes, etc., back on as a final touch. Pay attention to placement. Your quilt top is complete. Layer the quilt top, batting, and backing. Quilt and bind as desired.

Joni's Pathway

Joni's Story

Joni is a mixed-media artist and volunteer at a wild animal sanctuary. She is also mother to three adult children who have bounced in and out of her home with the flux of school, work, and relationships. Several years ago, Joni returned to her own childhood home to care for her aging mother. After her mother passed, Joni bought a smaller home but still ended up with a basement full of family treasures and extra everything.

With her creative eye and keen desire to reduce, reuse, and recycle where she can, Joni has been trying to reimagine items so that she and her family can continue to enjoy them. When cleaning out a particular closet, Joni was reluctant to throw away garments that weren't being used, but were still in decent shape—and carried memories to boot. When I asked if she had anything appropriate for my book project, she set aside two favorite shirts (one a comfy flannel, the other left behind by her youngest), a *yukata* (lightweight kimono) that had been a gift from a Japanese exchange student, and a work shirt from her eldest's first job.

After receiving the finished piece, she said:

> *I love the energetic colors and design of the table runner Kristin made. It adds a pop of color in my entryway and also reminds me of the loved ones who have passed through the doors in the houses where we've lived. I also feel good that we were able to save a few items from the landfill and give them new life as a useful object.*

The Pathway design was perfect for Joni as its crooked path represents how life rarely follows a straight line, but the unexpected turns can be intriguing and surprising.

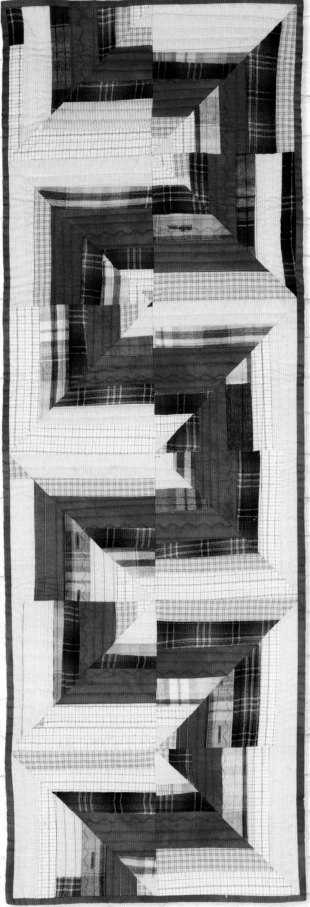

Pathway Table Runner

DIMENSIONS: 14" X 48" (35.6 X 121.9CM)

This table runner looks complicated, but the sewing is actually simple. It doesn't use a lot from each garment or special fabric, but does look best with a variety; along with being a small, quick project, it can also be a good second project for a collection of clothes. When arranging the strips, place the fabric that stands out the most (probably either the darkest or lightest, but maybe just a more colorful or bright one) next to the accent fabric.

YARDAGE
Special fabric: 5 shirts, approximately a sleeve or shirt front each
Accent fabric: ¼ yard (22.9cm)
Backing: 1½ yards (1.4m)
Binding: 1½ yards (1.4m)
Batting: 18" x 52" (45.7 x 132.1cm)

CUTTING
From accent fabric, cut:

(1) 2½" (6.4cm) x WOF strip, subcut into (2) 2½" x 22" (6.4 x 55.9cm) strips

(2) 2" (5.1cm) x WOF strips, subcut into (4) 2" x 22" (5.1 x 55.9cm) strips

From special fabrics, cut:

Strips anywhere between 1½"–3" (3.8–7.6cm) x 16" (40.6cm). If your special fabrics aren't long enough, sew another piece on the end. It's best if the pieced strips are close in color or value.

Assembly

Use a ¼" (6mm) seam allowance throughout.

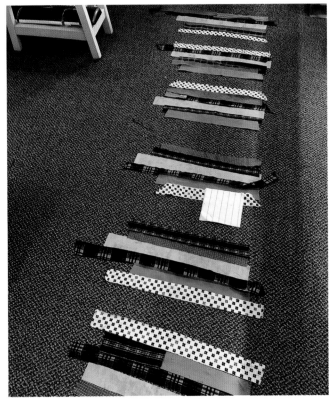

1. Arrange five to six special fabric strips around each accent strip. I like to leave my strips 16" (40.6cm) or a little longer at this point and trim after sewing.

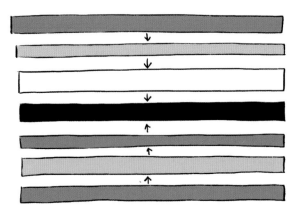

2. Sew a special fabric strip on each side of one accent strip. Add strips until the set is at least 8" (20.3cm) wide. The accent strip should remain about in the middle (shown in black on the diagram), but it doesn't need to be exact. Press seams open, especially if using denim.

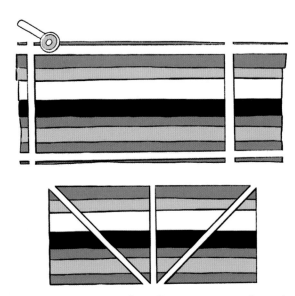

3. Trim the strip set to 8" x 16" (20.3 x 40.6cm). Cut in half to create two 8" x 8" (20.3 x 20.3cm) squares. Cut each square in half diagonally in *opposite directions* as in the diagram.

4. Repeat for each of the five remaining accent strips.

5. Pair triangles so that the strips create an L. Arrange to create a winding path similar to the diagram.

Plackets

Buttonhole plackets on shirts are great strips. These are the reinforced strips with the buttonholes in the very front of a shirt. I like to cut the shirt side of the placket ¼"–⅜" (0.6–1cm) from the placket itself. Sew this side of the strip as you would with any strip: right sides together, using a ¼" (6mm) seam allowance. The other, finished edge of the placket is too thick to make a nice seam, so I place it right sides up over the strip I want to sew it to, overlapping at least ¼" (6mm). Topstitch in place with a coordinating thread color. In the photo, the placket is topstitched to the dark plaid; the regular seam on the other side is sewn to the rust accent fabric.

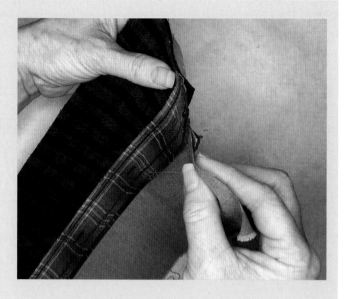

6. Pin the bias edges of each triangle pair. These edges stretch easily. The points of the triangles can easily get caught up in your machine's needle plate, so using leaders and enders (page 23) will help immensely. Sew carefully, and press the seam allowances open. A stiletto tool is helpful for holding seam allowances in place while sewing.

7. Chain-stitch each pair together. Press seam allowances in opposite directions. Sew rows together, nesting the seam allowances. Press seam allowances open or to each side.

8. Layer the table runner top, batting, and backing. For efficient use of your backing and binding fabric, cut the 1½ yards (1.4m) of backing fabric in half lengthwise. Use one half for the backing. From the other half, cut three lengthwise strips (2½" [6.4cm] wide) for the binding. Quilt and bind as desired.

Variation:
Patio Pillow

DIMENSIONS: 14" X 14" (35.6 X 35.6CM)

My friend Connie made this pillow out of old jeans and shirts, much like Joni's inspiration. She also had some denim in her stash with a great raveled (frayed) selvage. I love the way she used it to create a simple, overlapped envelope back for the pillow. Because this project looks best with a variety of special fabrics, but you don't need much of each, you may have a lot of unused fabric. This little project is a great option for a collection of garments that you want to share with more than one person, such as pillows for all the kids made from grandma's favorite dresses or aprons.

Assembly

1. Follow steps 1–3 of Pathway Table Runner (page 63). Make two strip sets, which will be cut into eight triangles. You will have accent fabric left over.

2. Arrange the triangles into a square as in the diagram.

YARDAGE

Special fabric: 5 shirts, approximately a sleeve or shirt front each

Accent fabric: ½ yard (45.7cm)

Backing: ½ yard (45.7cm)

Binding: ¼ yard (22.9cm)

Lining: 18" x 18" (45.7 x 45.7cm) muslin or scrap fabric

CUTTING

From accent fabric, cut:

(1) 2½" (6.4cm) x WOF strip, subcut into (2) 2½" x 22" (6.4 x 55.9cm) strips

(1) 2" (5.1cm) x WOF strip, subcut into (2) 2" x 22" (5.1 x 55.9cm) strips

From special fabrics, cut:

(12) strips anywhere between 1½"–3" (3.8–7.6cm) x 16" (40.6cm). If your special fabrics aren't long enough, sew another piece on the end. It's best if the pieced strips are close in color or value.

Optional: (2) 15" x 10" (38.1 x 25.4cm) rectangles for pillow back. The fabric should have a finished edge (either selvage or hemmed).

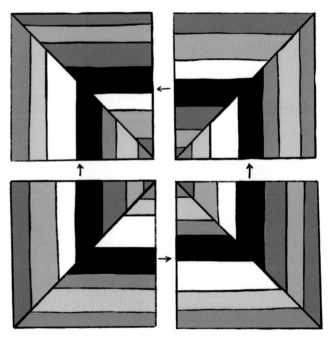

3. Sew triangles together into four squares. Press seams open to reduce bulk. Sew the square blocks together in pairs. Press seam allowances in opposite directions.

4. Sew the two pairs together. Press seams open. Sandwich with lining and batting and quilt as desired. Trim to 15" x 15" (38.1 x 38.1cm).

Pillow Back

5. Option 1: Finish the pillow as shown (right). Place the two 15" x 10" (38.1 x 25.4cm) rectangles on top of the pillow front, right sides together. Overlap the finished edges in the middle and ensure all perimeter edges are aligned. Sew around the perimeter with a ¼" (6mm) seam allowance. Turn the pillow right sides out through the opening created by the overlap.

6. Option 2: Finish with either Pillow Back 1 or 2 (pages 40 and 41). For Pillow Back 1, replace the 18½" (47cm) measurement with 15" (38.1cm). For Pillow Back 2, replace the rectangle dimensions with 15" x 6½" (38.1 x 16.5cm) and 15" x 11" (38.1 x 27.9cm).

Angela's Aspens

Angela's Story

Angela is an artist who picked up quilting again in 2016. She loves all types of fiber arts (crocheting, knitting, hand embroidery, etc.) and is a prolific reader. The last few years have been rough for Angela and her family. Her son had a leukemia relapse in 2013, and it all just snowballed until her mother's passing in 2021. Angela stood vigil next to two hospice beds, her son's then her mother's, and it was heavy.

Angela says she's just now taking steps out of her blanket fort, trying to go with the flow more and trying new things. She also wants to get back to working on her improv quilting. She saved a bag of clothes from her mother, Sandy, so that she could tackle making a memory quilt for her dad, and eventually a keepsake for herself and her brother. When she heard of this memory-quilt project, Angela thought it would be a great weight off her own shoulders as she knew it would still be some time before her creativity and emotions would meet in a place to sew this particular memory quilt.

Angela sent me a large box of her mother's clothes, many with beautiful elements around the necklines and hems. At first, I thought I might use all of the clothes, but as I cut and arranged the rectangles for the quilt, a smaller collection emerged that put the emphasis on the lovely details. Angela says of the quilt, "I love how you used the embroidered details front and center on some of the blocks. You really made the prints shine."

This finished quilt will go to Angela's dad. Her parents would have been married for 50 years on May 12, 2021. Her dad always says Sandy is the most beautiful women he knew. Angela wanted this memory quilt for her dad so he could have a "hug" whenever. She is confident he will cherish it.

Aspens Quilt

DIMENSIONS: 64" X 72" (1.6 X 1.8M)

I love the way the large rectangles on this quilt show off necklines and embellishments. There is no doubt that this quilt is made from beloved garments.

There are many techniques to make Flying Geese blocks (the wide triangles). This pattern uses a traditional method with one large rectangle for the "goose" and two smaller squares that are sewn on the diagonal for the background "sky." This allows you to cut the shapes from smaller parts of your special fabric and therefore have the most options for what you can use. I've given amounts below for all the Flying Geese elements to be created from purchased accent fabrics, but feel free to swap out several with your special fabrics. For example, Sandy's clothing included a solid hot pink tunic that called out to be the geese backgrounds. It wasn't quite enough, so I mixed in a pinkish striped shirt. Yardage amounts listed are enough for all the backgrounds to be the same.

Special Fabric Prep

If your garment has a nonrectangular detail, such as a decorative neckline, place a piece of fabric large enough to complete the rectangle under the neckline and topstitch it in place. Cut the rectangle to 8½" x 16½" (21.6 x 41.9cm). Trim away any excess fabric on the back.

To highlight an element like a front placket, remove the buttons (reattach them later, after quilting) and topstitch the placket in place.

Flying Geese

1. Pair two 4½" x 4½" (11.4 x 11.4cm) **K squares** with one 4½" x 8½" (11.4 x 21.6cm) **L rectangle**. Repeat with remaining background squares and geese rectangles.

YARDAGE

Special fabric: 6 shirts
Geese backgrounds: 1½ yards (1.4m), or two similarly colored shirts
Geese 1: ¼ yard (22.9cm), or one shirt back
Geese 2: ¼ yard (22.9cm), or one shirt back
Geese 3: ¼ yard (22.9cm), or one shirt back
Geese 4: ¼ yard (22.9cm), or one shirt back
Geese 5: ¼ yard (22.9cm), or one shirt back
Backing: 4 yards (3.7m)
Binding: ½ yard (45.7cm)
Batting: 68" x 76" (1.7 x 1.9m)

CUTTING

From special fabric, cut:
  (24) 8½" x 16½" (21.6 x 41.9cm) rectangles

  Optional: Replace any of the accent fabrics with special fabric, cut to the same sizes

From geese background, cut:
  (11) 4½" (11.4cm) x WOF strips, subcut into (70) 4½" x 4½" (11.4 x 11.4cm) squares for K

From geese accent fabrics, cut (from each):
  (1) 8½" (21.6cm) x WOF strip, subcut into (7) 8½" x 4½" (21.6 x 11.4cm) rectangles for L

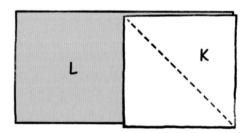

2. Draw a diagonal line on the back side of the K squares. Place one square, right sides together, on the right end of the L rectangle. The drawn diagonal line goes from the top center of the long side of the rectangle to the lower-right corner. Sew on the line. Press the lower-left corner of the square up to match the upper-right corner. Trim the excess underneath to a seam allowance of ¼" (6mm).

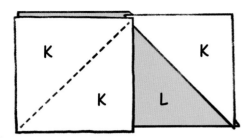

3. Place the second K square on the left end of the L rectangle, right sides together. The marked diagonal line goes from top center of the long side of the rectangle to the lower-left corner. The square should overlap the first triangle by ¼" (6mm). Sew together on the line. Press the lower-right corner of the square up to match the upper-left corner. Trim the excess underneath to a seam allowance of ¼" (6mm).

4. Repeat steps 2–3 for the remaining sets of geese rectangles and background squares.

Tip

Sewing just to the seam allowance side of the guideline will help to keep your blocks from shrinking to less than 8½" (21.6cm) wide after sewing on the background pieces.

Assembly

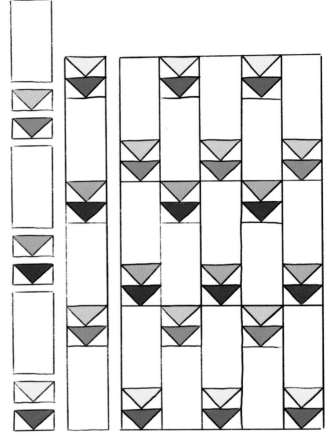

5. Arrange the 8½" x 16½" (21.6 x 41.9cm) rectangles and Flying Geese blocks following the diagram. Sew the blocks together in each vertical row. Press seams down. Sew the vertical rows together. Press seams in one direction. If seams are too thick to press in the instructed direction, it's okay to press them in the other.

6. Your quilt top is complete. Layer the quilt top, batting, and backing. Quilt and bind as desired. Sew patches, buttons, etc., back on as a final touch. Pay attention to placement.

Bonus Project

Gather the cut-off triangles from the Flying Geese blocks. Sew together the triangle pairs to make HSTs. They trim nicely to 3½" (8.9cm). Sew the HST blocks together to make a small quilt, wall hanging, or pillow, such as the HST Throw Pillow (page 54).

Constanze's Textile Art

Constanze's Story

Constanze is a textile artist, German by birth, Jewish by tradition, American by choice, and a fashion school dropout. She is currently living in New York with her husband and two kids. For this project, Constanze collected the clothes she wore over a few years in her early twenties. It was a tumultuous time in her life, full of trusting her heart over her fears and concerns.

In her words, the fabrics are:

- A skirt and apron from a dirndl I wore before our move (the trying-to-make-Germany-work phase)

- A light blue blouse (my mom bought for me for my first job in Germany)

- A striped blouse (I bought myself for my first job in New York)

- Two aprons (my mother-in-law bought as an anniversary present after our move)

- Table linens from our first place in New York

- A tote bag I used for art school in New York (bought on a visit back to Germany)

Constanze met her husband before she had chosen a career or a place to live.

> He accompanied me not just on the journey of immigration, but also trying out fashion school, finding that it wasn't what I had hoped for, and finding a place for art in my life nonetheless. From a dirndl worn in Germany, to a paint-stained bag I wore to class, to one of my first Corporate Job shirts, these fabrics hold memories of how I learned who I wanted to be and remind me of the love that carried me through it all.

Constanze has made a lot of memory quilts over the years and loves how a textile can always transport us back in time, bring back loved ones, or bring back our past selves. Even though she had made many memory pieces for others, and had put this set of clothes aside a while ago, she could never quite visualize what she wanted to do with them. Handing these treasured memories over to me was a way to get a new perspective, both objective and knowing my story. Constanze says, "It feels like a permission to talk about these years that I had not quite felt before."

These artworks are going on the wall! Like with most memory quilts, Constanze is excited to point to them when her kids get older and talk about these formative years before they were born. Looking at these fabrics always makes Constanze appreciate why she and her husband chose this path that they are on.

Flock Wall Art

Special garments don't need to be turned into quilts for the bed. Perhaps you want to make several smaller things to gift to multiple family members. Or maybe the textiles are too delicate or dear to withstand daily use. Maybe you just want a smaller project. Mounting a small, quilted piece onto an inexpensive stretched canvas, or stretcher bars purchased from the art supply store at specific lengths, creates unique and meaningful art to hang on the wall and enjoy daily.

In this wall art, lots of tiny HST units surround a center that shows off a colorful fabric, like Constanze's floral, or a detail on a meaningful T-Shirt. Choose one solid color for your HST accent and it will tie together as many garments as you like. Constanze had a light blue chambray shirt that fit this use perfectly, but you may need to purchase a solid fabric that coordinates with your center.

YARDAGE

Special fabric: 2 shirts (but more is better), approximately one sleeve or front each
Accent fabric: ⅔ yard (61cm), or one shirt
Batting: 28" x 28" (71.1 x 71.1cm)
Backing: ¾ yard (68.6cm) muslin or scrap fabric

CUTTING

From special fabric, cut:

(1) 8½" x 8½" (21.6 x 21.6cm) square for the center

(64) 3½" x 3½" (8.9 x 8.9cm) squares, from a variety of special fabrics

From accent fabric, cut:

(6) 3½" (8.9cm) x WOF strips, subcut into (64) 3½" x 3½" (8.9 x 8.9cm) squares

Assembly

1. Pair each accent square, right sides together, with a 3½" x 3½" (8.9 x 8.9cm) **special fabric square.** Following the instructions on page 25, create 128 HSTs. Trim each HST block to 2½" x 2½" (6.4 x 6.4cm) if necessary.

2. Arrange the HST units into pleasing groups of four **across and four down.** This will create eight blocks. I rotated the direction of a few units to break up the repetition and add a bit of interest. Sew each group together, pressing the seam allowances open or nested.

3. Arrange the eight blocks around the 8½" x 8½" (21.6 x 21.6cm) **square as shown.** Sew the groups together in rows. Then sew the rows together. Press well.

4. Sandwich the top, batting, and backing. Quilt as desired. If you have used starch or another product that should be washed out, gently soak your project and dry flat on a towel. Once dry, iron flat and trim to 24" x 24" (61 x 61cm).

5. Mount to canvas (page 85) or frame as desired.

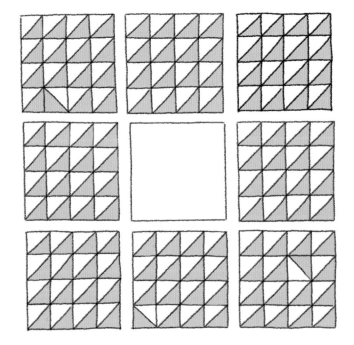

Hearth Wall Art

DIMENSIONS: 24" X 24" (61 X 61CM)

Hearth uses a variation of a Log Cabin. One or two solid accent fabrics will pull together three or four special fabrics. Again, Constanze's plain shirt stood in for a purchased solid. The navy blue eyelet table linen is also simple enough to do the work of a solid. Your choices may or may not need purchased solids. Choose an interesting print or a logo or special detail from a shirt for the center square, then work your way out, adding solid fabric if necessary to give the eye a rest from busier prints and stripes or to tie the color scheme together.

Flying Geese

Use ¼" (6mm) seam allowance throughout.

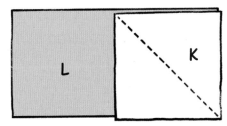

1. Draw a diagonal line on the back sides of the K squares. Pay attention to the direction if using stripes. Place one square, right sides together, on the right end of one L rectangle. The drawn line goes from the top center of the L rectangle to the lower-right corner. Sew on the drawn line. Press the lower-left corner of the square up to match the upper-right corner. Trim the excess underneath to a seam allowance of ¼" (6mm).

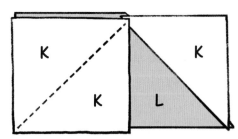

2. Place another K square, right sides together, on the left end of the L rectangle. The drawn line goes from top center of the long side of the L rectangle to the lower-left corner. The square should overlap the first triangle by ¼" (6mm). Sew on the drawn line. Press the lower-right corner of the square up to match the upper-left corner. Repeat for the other three L rectangles for a total of four Flying Geese units. Set aside.

YARDAGE

Special fabric: 1–4 shirts
Accent fabric: ⅛–¼ yard (11.4–22.9cm) for each round
Batting: 28" x 28" (71.1 x 71.1cm)
Backing: ¾ yard (68.6cm) muslin or scrap fabric

CUTTING

From special OR accent fabric, cut:

(1) 4½" x 4½" (11.4 x 11.4cm) square for A

(2) 2½" x 4½" (6.4 x 11.4cm) rectangles for B

(2) 2½" x 8½" (6.4 x 21.6cm) rectangles for C

(2) 3½" x 8½" (8.9 x 21.6cm) for rectangles D

(2) 3½" x 14½" (8.9 x 36.8cm) rectangles for E

(3) 1" x 3½" (2.5 x 8.9cm) contrasting strips for E inserts

(2) 1½" x 14½" (3.8 x 36.8cm) strips for F

(2) 1½" x 16½" (3.8 x 41.9cm) strips for G

(1) 4½" x 10½" (11.4 x 26.7cm) rectangle for H

(1) 4½" x 14½" (11.4 x 36.8cm) rectangle for I

(2) 4½" x 24½" (11.4 x 62.2cm) rectangles for J

(8) 2½" x 2½" (6.4 x 6.4cm) squares for K

(4) 2½" x 4½" (6.4 x 11.4cm) contrasting rectangles for L

Log Cabin

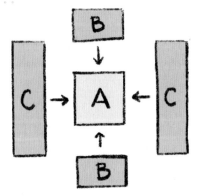

3. Round one: Sew the B rectangles to the top and bottom of the center A square. Press away from the center. Sew the C rectangles to the sides of the BAB unit as shown. Press away from the center.

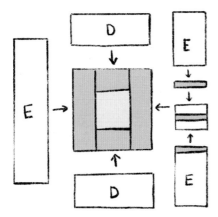

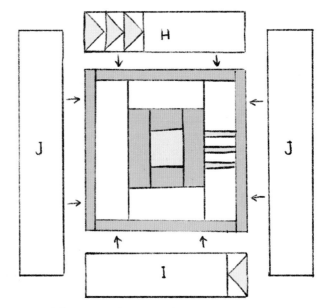

4. Round two: Sew the D rectangles to the top and bottom of the ABC unit. Press away from the center. Sew one E rectangle to the left side of the ABCD unit. Press away from the center.

5. Cut the remaining E rectangle in half crosswise. Sew a 1" x 3½" (2.5 x 8.9cm) insert strip in between the two halves. Press seams open. Cut the reconstructed rectangle again, 1¼" (3.2cm) above the insert; sew in another insert strip, pressing seams open. Then cut the reconstructed rectangle again, 1¼" (3.2cm) below the first; center, insert, and sew in the third insert strip, pressing seams open. Trim the reconstructed E rectangle to 3½" x 14½" (8.9 x 36.8cm) if necessary. Sew to the right side of the ABCD unit. Press seams away from the center.

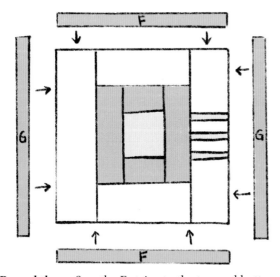

6. Round three: Sew the F strips to the top and bottom of the ABCDE unit. Press away from the center. Sew the G strips to the sides of the ABCDEF unit as shown. Press away from the center.

7. Round four: Sew three KL Flying Geese units in a row along their long sides. Sew the H rectangle to the point end of the Flying Geese unit. Trim the KLH strip to 4½" x 16½" (11.4 x 41.9cm) if necessary. Sew to the top of the ABCDEFG unit. Press seam allowances toward the center.

8. Sew the remaining KL Flying Geese unit to the I rectangle. Point the goose to the right end of the rectangle. Sew the constructed strip to the bottom of the ABCDEFGH unit. Press seam allowances toward the center.

9. Sew the J rectangles to the sides of the ABCDEFGHI unit. Press the seams toward the center.

Assembly

10. Sandwich the top, batting, and backing. Quilt as desired. If you have used starch or another product that should be washed out, gently soak your project and dry flat on a towel. Once dry, iron flat and trim to 24" x 24" (61 x 61cm).

11. Mount to canvas (page 85) or frame as desired.

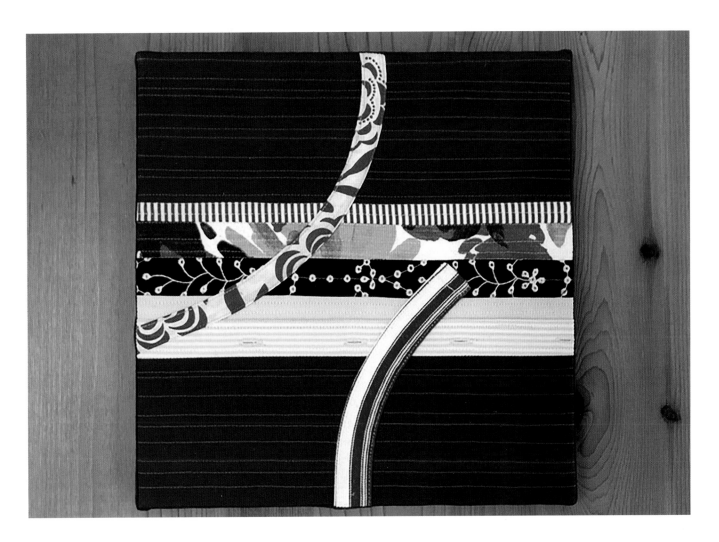

Arcs Wall Art

DIMENSIONS: 12" X 12" (30.5 X 30.5CM)

This small art quilt is perfect for smaller bits and interesting details. Even mundane parts like T-Shirt collars add a dynamic element to this simple composition. I used a buttonhole placket as a stripe on Constanze's Arc and straps from an apron and a tote bag to make the arcs themselves. For Kenny's Arc, I used T-shirt collars for the arcs and the raw edge of an opened-up denim seam for a textural stripe. Be creative—how about a glittery bit of a party dress for a stripe, or wedding lace for the arcs?

YARDAGE

Special fabric: 6 different scraps, at least 1" x 12½" (2.5 x 31.8cm)
Background fabric: 1 Fat Quarter
Batting: 16" x 16" (40.6 x 40.6cm)
Backing: ½ yard (45.7cm) muslin or scrap fabric

CUTTING

From special fabrics, cut:
Strips anywhere between 1"–3" (2.5–7.6cm) x 12½" (31.8cm), enough that their finished widths add up to 4" (10.2cm) (e.g., four strips, 1½" [3.8cm] wide; or three strips, 1½" [3.8cm] wide, plus two strips, 1" [2.5cm] wide). Remember the finished width is ½" (1.3cm) less than when you cut them.

(1) 12" x ¾" (30.5 x 1.9cm) strip for arc 1

(1) 7¾" x 1" (19.7 x 2.5cm) strip for arc 2

From background fabric, cut:
(2) 4½" x 12½" (11.4 x 31.8cm) rectangles

Assembly

Use ¼" (6mm) seam allowances throughout.

1. Arrange the special fabric strips in a pleasing order.
Sew together along their long edges, right sides together.
Press seam allowances open. If you want to show off an
interesting raw edge or have an already-finished edge (such
as a placket), you can overlap one strip next to another by
½" (1.3cm), right sides up, and topstitch in place. Trim the
strip set to 4½" x 12½" (11.4 x 31.8cm) if necessary.

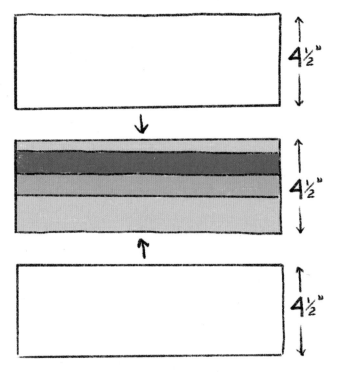

**2. Sew a background rectangle to each side of the strip
set.** Press seams toward the background.

3. Sandwich the quilt top with batting only. Quilt
as desired.

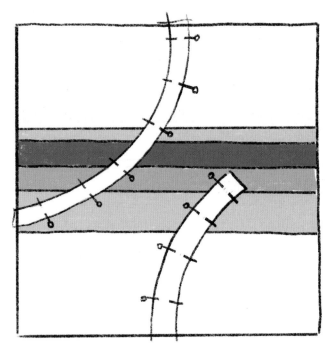

4. Pin arcs to the quilt top as in diagram. I used fabric
with an already-finished edge, such as collars and apron
straps. If needed, before attaching to the quilt top, fold
each raw edge ¼" (6mm) under and stitch ⅛" (3mm) from
the edge. You can also leave edges raw if desired. Stitch arcs
to the quilt top by machine or by hand.

5. Sandwich the top and batting to the backing. Quilt
more if desired, or just baste around the edges. If you have
used starch or another product that should be washed out,
gently soak your project and dry flat on a towel. Once dry,
iron flat and trim to 12½" x 12½" (31.8 x 31.8cm).

6. Mount to canvas (page 85) or frame as desired.

Grow Wall Art

DIMENSIONS: 12" X 12" (30.5 X 30.5CM)

This small art quilt is perfect for smaller bits and interesting details. There is ample opportunity for embellishment, especially if you enjoy hand embroidery. I added buttons from one of Constanze's shirts, simple embroidery with perle cotton floss, and the couching stitch (page 85) with a coordinating yarn for a bolder line. Be creative—go ahead and layer fancy fabrics if you've got them, or let those flannel shirts fray at the edges. Feel free to mix up where the special fabrics and the accent fabric are used—maybe you want to concentrate the special fabric in the center of the composition and frame it with a solid color on each side.

Assembly

Use ¼" (6mm) seam allowances throughout.

1. Spend some time layering and arranging your fabrics to find a pleasing order. Decide which fabric will be the center strip and which will be sewn on each side. The rest of the fabrics (that form the abstract flower in the center) will be added on, collage style.

YARDAGE AND SUPPLIES

Special fabric: 1 main shirt, plus scraps from several others

Background fabric: 1 Fat Quarter, or ¼ yard (22.9cm)

Batting: 16" x 16" (40.6 x 40.6cm)

Backing: ½ yard (45.7cm) muslin or scrap fabric

Embroidery thread, various colors

Yarn

CUTTING

From special fabrics, cut:

    (2) 4½" x 12½" (11.4 x 31.8cm) rectangles for sides

    (1) 5" x 5" (12.7 x 12.7cm) square for bottom flower

    (1) 3" x 3" (7.6 x 7.6cm) square for middle flower

    (1) 1½" x 1½" (3.8 x 3.8cm) square for top flower

    (1) 5" x 2" (12.7 x 5.1cm) rectangle for stem

From background fabric, cut:

    (1) 4½" x 12½" (11.4 x 31.8cm) rectangle for center

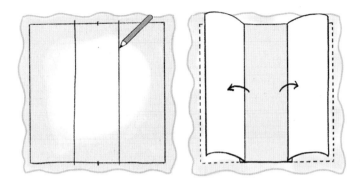

2. Mark a 12½" x 12½" (31.8 x 31.8cm) square on the batting with a marking tool. I like to construct this piece directly on the batting as it adds stabilization for the embellishments. Find and mark the center at the top and bottom of the square. Measure 2¼" (5.7cm) to both the left and right of each center mark. Draw two vertical lines connecting the top and bottom marks, using a tool that won't show through your fabrics. Lay your center fabric between the two lines, face up. Place one of your side fabrics face down on the right side of the center fabric and sew in place. Repeat for the left side. Press side fabrics away from the center.

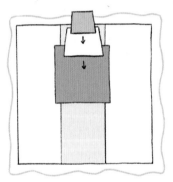

3. Layer your "flower" fabrics. Arrange above the stem fabric. The pieces can vary depending on what looks best with your fabrics. Use a glue stick (sparingly) to hold them in place. Quilt, if desired, through the fabrics and the batting.

Running Stitch

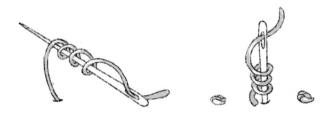

French Knot

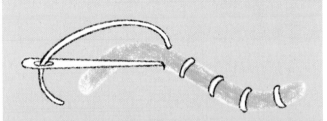

Couching Stitch

Couching is a great way to add a thick yarn or ribbon that is too large to fit through a needle or won't stand up to the stress of stitching. Lay the yarn to be couched on top of your base fabric. You can arrange it as you go or use a little fabric glue to hold it in place (just a few dots in strategic places). Use a sewing thread in a matching color and bring the needle up on one side of the yarn and down on the other side. Bring the needle back up about ⅛" (3mm) in front of the previous stitch and back down on the other side. Continue until all the yarn is secured to the base fabric. If desired, leave a long tail of yarn at the beginning and the end of the design and thread it though a large-eyed needle and pull it to the back side of the fabric.

4. Use the embroidery stitches of your choice to embellish and further secure the collaged fabrics. I used a running stitch along the outside edge of the bottom and middle flower square. I also added French knots along the outside edge of the top flower square. Add buttons if desired.

5. Use a water- or air-soluble pen to draw a squiggly "flower" on each side section. I made the total height 6" (15.2cm) from the bottom, with the squiggle starting about 4½" (11.4cm) up. Couch yarn (see above) or embroider the design as desired.

6. Sandwich the top and batting to the backing. Quilt more if desired, or just baste around the edges. If you have used starch or another product that should be washed out, gently soak your project and dry flat on a towel. Once dry, iron flat and trim to 12½" x 12½" (31.8 x 31.8cm).

7. Mount to canvas (page 85) or frame as desired.

Waterfall Wall Art

DIMENSIONS: 18" X 24" (45.7 X 61CM)

The long strips in this design are perfect for showing off a collection of crazy ties, but it would work just as well as a subtle collection of dress shirts, especially if several front plackets were included. I used a nubby silk as the solid-color accent to match the silkiness of Art's tie collection. Cotton or velvet would work just as well. If you are using T-shirts, consider using denim for your accent squares!

YARDAGE
Special fabric: 9 ties or 2 shirts (but more is better), approximately one sleeve each
Accent fabric: 1 Fat Quarter
Batting: 22" x 28" (55.9 x 71.1cm)
Backing: ⅝ yard (57.2cm) muslin or scrap fabric

CUTTING
From special fabrics, cut:
    (9) 2½" x 18½" (6.4 x 47cm) strips

    (14) 2½" x 2½" (6.4 x 6.4cm) squares

From accent fabric, cut:
    (13) 2½" x 2½" (6.4 x 6.4cm) squares

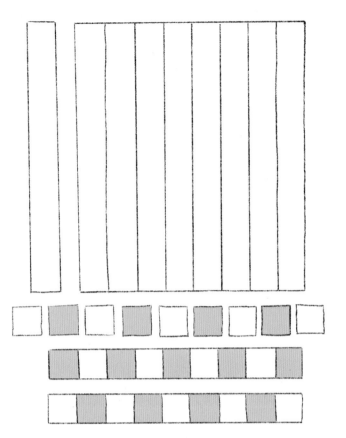

Assembly

1. Arrange the strips in a pleasing order. Sew together. Press seam allowances open.

2. Arrange the squares in a checkerboard. Alternate the special-fabric and the accent-fabric squares. Be mindful of the row joining to the strip section to avoid pairing up matching fabrics. Sew together in rows, then sew the rows together. Press seams open or use nesting seams.

3. Sew the strip section to the checkerboard section. Press well.

4. Sandwich the top, batting, and backing. Quilt as desired. If you have used starch or another product that should be washed out, gently soak your project and dry flat on a towel. Once dry, iron flat and trim to 18½" x 24½" (47 x 62.2cm).

5. Mount to canvas (page 85) or frame as desired.

Art's Story

The youngest of four, Art always considered himself to be a bit of a rebel, but his first few jobs out of college were at a stuffy government office that required a suit and tie. So he amassed a collection of wacky ties to defy the conservative fashion choices of those around him. Art went on to join the army and wear a uniform for the next 20 years, but he kept his tie collection as a reminder of his personal style. Now retired, he'll probably never wear the ties again, so we chose a few in similar color palettes to make a wall hanging with a bohemian vibe.

I love that every day I see the colors and patterns of my ties and they remind me of places and events, like the food tie for all the yummy restaurants I enjoyed in DC, and the elephant tie which nods to my poli-sci background. It pleases me that my collection is no longer hidden away at the back of the closet.

Mounting on Canvas

YARDAGE AND SUPPLIES

Edge fabric: ⅓ yard (30.5cm), can be the same as the accent fabric or a coordinating color

Canvas and hanging hardware (dimensions indicated on each project)

Staple gun

Twill tape (optional)

CUTTING

From edge fabric, cut:

2 strips, the length of your canvas x the depth of your canvas or stretcher bars, plus 1" (2.5cm)

2 strips, the width of your canvas x the depth of your canvas or stretcher bars, plus 1" (2.5cm)

Assembly

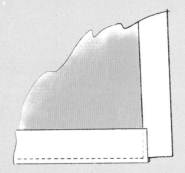

1. Place two edge strips on opposite sides of the quilt, right sides together. Sew with a ¼" (6mm) seam allowance. Start ¼" (6mm) from the beginning of each strip and stop ¼" (6mm) from the end. Press away from the quilt. Repeat with the remaining edge strips on the top and bottom of the quilt. The seams should meet at the corners but not cross. Press away from the quilt.

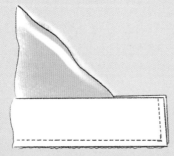

2. At one corner, match the short ends of the side strips. Fold the quilt out of the way. Sew from the outer edge to the side seam intersection.

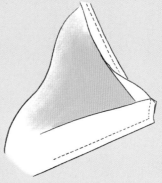

3. Repeat for each corner. The edge strips should be perpendicular to the quilt, not flat.

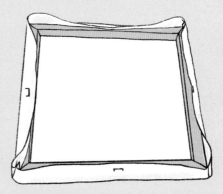

4. Slip the quilt over the canvas or assembled stretcher bars. Gently wrap the side strips to the back of the canvas. Staple in place using a staple gun. Start with one staple in the center of each side back and work toward the corners, making sure that the quilt is centered on the front.

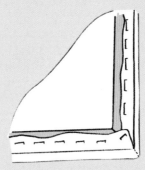

5. When you reach the corners, fold them as flat as you can like wrapping a present. Staple in place.

6. Optional: Cover the raw fabric edges on the back of the canvas. Use a length of twill tape glued in place with tacky glue or hot glue.

7. Add hanging hardware and enjoy!

Art's Portal

Art's Story

Art is an appreciator of quilts and is basically the inspiration for this book. He's my husband of more than 27 years—20 of those as an active-duty army officer. When he was first commissioned as a second lieutenant, I made him a red, white, and blue quilt with stars and stripes that is still well used. Throughout the years, knowing my love of fabric, Art would give me his old uniforms whenever he purchased a new one. I have incorporated pieces of these into my art quilts to help tell the story of our army family, in which moves, deployments, and uncertainty are always present. When Art retired, I made this Portal quilt to honor the occasion. That inspired me to make more quilts for our military friends as they retired, and then to seek to share those patterns (and more!) as a book so readers can create their own stories in special fabric.

For Art and me, Portal represents a transition from one place or period to another. We didn't know where retirement would take him, but we were excited to figure it out. I see the abstract arches in the quilt as doorways or passages to something new or different. Each color is a phase traveled through. The gold and bronze embroidered stars stand in for all the awards Art received during the years he served.

This will be added to Art's growing quilt collection: the first one I made him, a gift from a Girl Scout troop, a Quilt of Valor, and now Portal. Each of these treasured quilts holds a special meaning and marks a period in his career and in his life.

Portal Quilt

DIMENSIONS: 48" X 54" (121.9 X 137.2CM)

This pattern will create a lap-sized quilt reminiscent of a doorway or passage. Utilize special fabrics, such as a uniform, a collection of shirts, baby clothes, etc. You'll cut and arrange the fabrics according to the amounts you have. Even though the quilt is on the small size, most of the pieces are larger than a typical garment; in most cases, you will have to first cut rectangles and squares from your special fabrics and sew them together to create the necessary long strips in this design. This is a good design if you have jeans or other pants in your collection.

Each "portal" should have fabrics that are similar in color and value so that they read as a cohesive piece. The thin accent portal should be different or contrasting in color. For any other portals, choose colors found in your special fabric and maybe a neutral for the outermost portal.

YARDAGE

Center: ¼ yard (22.9cm)
First portal: ½ yard (45.7cm), or 1–2 shirts
Second portal: ½ yard (45.7cm), or 1–2 shirts
Third portal (accent fabric): ¼ yard (22.9cm)
Fourth portal: ⅝ yard (57.2cm), or 2–3 shirts
Fifth portal: 1½ yards (1.4m)
Binding: ½ yard (45.7cm)
Backing: 3⅛ yards (2.9m)
Batting: 52" x 58" (1.3 x 1.5m)

CUTTING

From center fabric, cut:
  (1) 4½" (11.4cm) x WOF strip, subcut into (1) 4½" x 26½" (11.4 x 67.3cm) for A*

From first portal fabric, cut:
  (2) 4½" x 26½" (11.4 x 67.3cm) strips for B*

  (1) 6½" x 12" (16.5 x 30.5cm) rectangle for C

From second portal fabric, cut:
  (2) 4½" (11.4cm) x WOF strips, subcut into (2) 4½" x 32½" (11.4 x 82.6cm) for D*

  (1) 4½" (11.4cm) x WOF strip, subcut into (1) 4½" x 20½" (11.4 x 52.1cm) rectangle for E*

From accent fabric, cut:
  (2) 2½" (6.4cm) x WOF strips, subcut into (2) 2½" x 36½" (6.4 x 92.7cm) for F

  (1) 2½" (6.4cm) x WOF strip, subcut into (1) 2½" x 24½" (6.4 x 62.2cm) rectangle for G

From fourth portal fabric, cut:
  (2) 4½" (11.4cm) x WOF strips, subcut into (2) 4½" x 38½" (11.4 x 97.8cm) rectangles for H*

  (1) 8½" (21.6cm) x WOF strip, subcut to (1) 8½" x 32½" (21.6 x 82.6cm) rectangle for I**

From fifth portal fabric, cut:
  (2) 8½" (21.6cm) x length of fabric strips, subcut into (2) 8½" x 46½" (21.6 x 118.1cm) rectangles for J

  (1) 8½" (21.6cm) x length of fabric strip, subcut into (1) 8½" x 48½" (21.6 x 123.2cm) rectangle for K

* If cutting from special fabric, piece enough 4½" (11.4cm) strips as needed into the indicated size

** If cutting from special fabric, piece enough 8½" (21.6cm) strips as needed into the indicated size

Assembly

Use ¼" (6mm) seam allowance throughout.

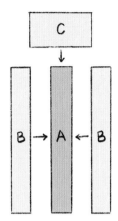

1. Sew one B strip to each side of the center A strip. Press seams. Sew the C rectangle to the top of BAB. Press seams away from the center.

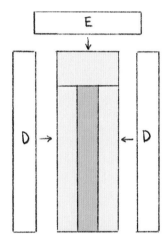

2. Sew one D strip to each long side of ABC. Press seams. Sew the E rectangle to the top of ABCD. Press seams away from the center.

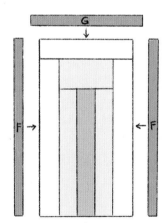

3. Sew one F accent strip to each long side of ABCDE. Press seams. Sew the G accent strip to the top end of ABCDEF. Press seams away from the center.

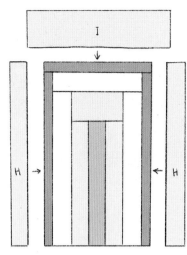

4. Sew one H strip to each long side of ABCDEFG. Press seams. Sew the I rectangle to the top of ABCDEFGH. Press seams away from the center.

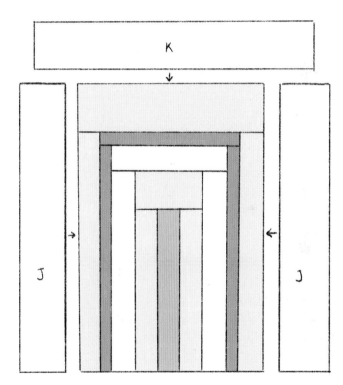

5. Sew one J strip to each long side of ABCDEFGHI. Press seams. Sew the K strip to the top end of ABCDEFGHIJ. Press seams away from the center.

6. Your quilt top is complete. Layer the quilt top, batting, and backing. Quilt and bind as desired. Sew patches, nametapes, etc., back on as a final touch. Pay attention to placement.

Eden's Cairn

Eden's Story

Eden is a lifelong Northern Californian, a second-generation Mexican, the first in her family to go to graduate school, a Generation X woman, a second-generation pediatric critical care nurse, a pediatric nurse practitioner, a moderately skilled home chef and baker, and crafty curious. She is the product of a 1960s romance straight out of Vietnam War–era Berkeley where the lives of a two-tour vet and a liberal, worldly college student full of dreams from Madison, Wisconsin, collided. Though it was never Eden's life goal to become a nurse—an occupation that historically has been a trade requiring on-the-job training, as opposed to a well-educated and respected "profession"—26 years later, here Eden still is, making a difference in the lives of critically ill children and making an impact on the world, if not in the way her mother had envisioned.

> *Honestly in the end, I have a very robust, interesting, and successful career. I have been working with people in the throes of personal crisis my entire career. A large portion of my population has been sick babies and kids and their families, who undoubtedly were experiencing the worst days of their lives. These days (maybe it has been always?) when I am with my patients I am in my element; my cape of confidence is flying strong, my skills are sharp, my experience is vast, my mind focused. I spend a lot of hours of my life at work, with the sick babies and kids and their families, who are experiencing pain, despair, loneliness, grief. In addition, being in medicine requires the ability to get dirty at any notice; lay on the ground, get bodily fluids doused on you, run down the hall, jump over a fence—literally—hold a crying baby, prepare a meal, go to the morgue. All of this requiring easy-fitting, sturdy, protective, cute attire.*

When I thought about creating a memory quilt to commemorate a moment in time, I thought about Eden and her experience as a health care worker during the COVID-19 pandemic. The project is a memento mori of sorts. It recognizes the sacrifices Eden and millions of other health care workers have made through unprecedented times.

The term "scrubs" literally came from hospital-provided utility garments that operating room clinicians would wear when they "scrubbed in." They were cut from two identical pieces of the same fabric and sandwiched together for front and back, tops and bottoms. They were reversible, unisex, shapeless utility garments devoid of ornamentation or pockets, putrid seafoam green with the hospital name stamped on the chest or backside. Modern-day nurses like Eden have strayed away from the historically all-white uniforms denoting sterility and cleanliness and now have a more athletic and "casual" vibe. Occasionally, one can spot someone sporting the free *or* modern scrubs in public, which some amount to strutting a status or announcing professional superiority. Darker colors reign supreme, and the ability to express individuality through style and pattern is more widely accepted. Eden now realizes that she almost *never* wears her "scrubs," work jackets, or anything "nursing-y" in public, supposing when she's in her scrubs she is in a hyper-focused work state of mind, so it never occurs to her to go anywhere else besides the hospital in them. At home, her scrubs, work vests, and jackets are in a separate dresser with their own set of specific matching undershirts and socks with specific shoes. They have their own persona and purpose, saturated with memories, spirits, tears, blood, and coffee. She notes her cool-ish nurse flight suit and transport-nurse uniforms feel silly "in the wild."

> *When Kristin asked if I'd be willing to have some of my scrubs made into a quilt or table runner, I was surprised at how emotionally attached I was to items that are merely "work attire." It never occurred to me that my uniforms could be something of reverence or beauty. In and of themselves, the garments are obviously made of fabric that hold their own weight and personality. When the pieces are separated from the implied utility and the perspective is changed, they take on entirely under-realized meanings.*
>
> *Odd to say that I feel like it says that when I wear my scrubs, I am just a worker bee in a sea of bees, but having pieces of them immortalized as art is announcing that the work I do on a daily basis is important and recognized. I have never felt as though anyone is proud of Eden the Nurse. The quilt whispers this to me though.*

Eden enjoys her work and it fulfills her, so it was satisfying to me to create something through which she can see herself—shape-shifted into fabric, as she said. A beautifully crafted piece to reflect the gratitude and self-worth she has earned through her years of dedication.

> *It is such a gift to experience the beginning of life and the last breath of a human, even more of a child. It is humbling to know that I have the capacity to revive a stopped heart and have been successful many times over; it is a gift to be able to give back life to families, to parents, and dreadfully sad when the outcome is not expected or intended. When I am alone with a person that has died, I feel comfort that their spirit has moved on to a new life hopefully free of pain and suffering. Life is fragile and we ought to make the most out of every moment we are alive. This quilt has pieces of scrubs I have worn at the end of a life. I remember these little young lives through your creative hands and heart. Interesting that fabric of my old scrubs, that lived in their own separate drawer away from my "real-life" attire, pieced together in an artful arrangement, can evoke so many feelings and wonderment. That old uniforms can create an internal contemplative dialogue, a flood of emotions.*

For Eden, this quilt piece feels like a spotlight shining down on her success as a nurse, for the first time ever. Not knowing what I'd ultimately create, she was surprised by the idea of hanging the quilt on the wall. Not only does it showcase an interesting and modern design with striking colors, within it the piece holds a secret meaning and emotions only Eden can relate to. It says, "You have done good, girl from Berkeley. Be proud of the lives you have touched; you and your work matter."

Cairn Table Runner

DIMENSIONS: 16" X 53" (40.6 X 134.6CM)

The solid colors of Eden's scrubs lend themselves nicely to the mid-century modern vibe of the Cairn design, especially with the small accent of a handmade mask and surgical cap. But it would also look great with small prints. Don't let the curves scare you—glue-basting makes them much easier than you might think. (Thank you Jen Carlton-Bailly for making me a convert!) The organic design of the table runner means that even if your curves aren't perfect, the design still works.

Read the preparation sidebar (see page 94) before cutting. The cutting list refers to the colors in Eden's project, so you can easily compare which fabric goes with which letter. Make notes of your colors.

YARDAGE AND SUPPLIES

Glue stick

Thin cardboard (such as a cereal box), or template plastic

Marking tools (such as a pencil, Pilot FriXion erasable pen, or chalk pencil/liner)

Purchased fabric: ⅜ yard (34.3cm)

Special fabrics: 5 shirts, plus 2 optional scraps or small items (such as a mask or scrub cap)

Binding: ⅓ yard (30.5cm)

Backing: 1 yard (91.4cm) (1⅓ yard [121.9cm] if quilting with a long-armer and you need extra inches around the edges)

Batting: 20" x 57" (50.8 x 144.8cm)

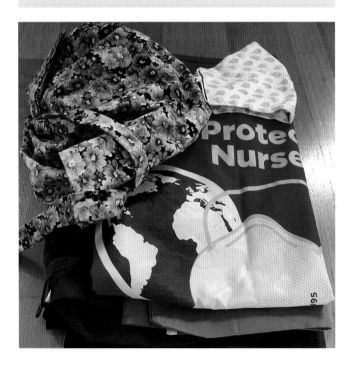

CUTTING

From purchased fabric (pale yellow solid fabric), cut:

    (1) 8½" x 2½" (21.6 x 6.4cm) rectangle for top border 1

    3 AA shapes

    4 AA shapes, reversed

    1 BB shape

    1 BB shape, reversed

    1 CC shape

From special fabric 1 (royal blue scrubs), cut:

    (1) 8½" x 2½" (21.6 x 6.4cm) rectangle for top border 2

    2 AA shapes

    1 AA shape, reversed

    2 BB shapes

    2 BB shapes, reversed

    1 CC shape

    2 CC shapes, reversed

From special fabric 2 (kelly green scrubs), cut:

    (1) 16½" x 2½" (41.9 x 6.4cm) rectangle for bottom border

    1 A shape, reversed

    1 B shape, reversed

    2 AA shapes

    2 AA shapes, reversed

From special fabric 3 (light teal scrubs), cut:

    1 A shape

    3 A shapes, reversed

    1 B shape, reversed

    1 B shape, reversed

    2 C shapes

From special fabric 4 (red scrubs), cut:

    1 A shape

    2 A shapes, reversed

    1 B shape

    1 B shape, reversed

From special fabric 5 (black scrubs), cut:

    3 A shapes

    1 A shape, reversed

    2 C shapes, reversed

From special fabric (bonus scraps or small items), cut:

    1 A shape

    1 B shape

Preparation

Create templates for the curved pieces by following the QR code on page 102. You can download the templates and print them out at home or through a print store. My favorite method is to make copies of the template pages and glue them to thin cardboard such as a cereal box. Cut out the shapes with an X-Acto knife. If you have template plastic, you can trace the shapes directly onto the plastic and then cut them out. Use a straight edge for the straight sides.

Determine which shapes you will cut out of which color. It is helpful to tape a small swatch or make a note on the pattern as to which will be Fabric 2, Fabric 3, etc. Trace around each shape onto your fabric. Pay attention to the grainline of the fabric and place your templates so the straight edges are either parallel or perpendicular to the grain. Using templates allows you to cut the shapes from odd pieces, like sleeves and yokes, and to maximize how many shapes you can cut—but care needs to be taken not to place the shapes on the bias just to make it fit. I like to cut the straight lines using my rotary ruler on the traced lines, then cut the curves with just a small rotary cutter or scissors. Cut each shape and mark the notch with a marking tool or a snip with your scissors (within the seam allowance). The A and B pieces look similar once cut out, so it is helpful to keep them in separate, labeled baggies until you sew them to their backgrounds.

Arc Blocks

Use a ¼" (6mm) seam allowance throughout.

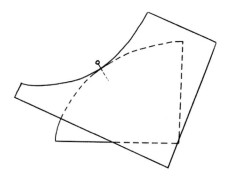

1. Match the first arc to its background. Set the pair on a flat surface with the background shape on top of the arc shape, right sides together. Pin the pieces together at the notch.

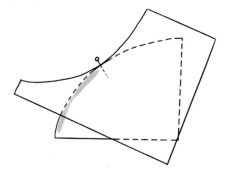

2. Dab glue along the curved edge of the arc. Only place from the pin to one edge.

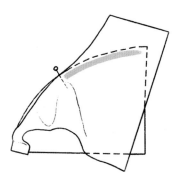

3. Stick the corresponding edge of the background piece in place. Match straight ends. Gently ease the concave curve of the background piece into place along the convex curve of the arc. Make sure it's smooth ¼" (6mm) from the raw edge.

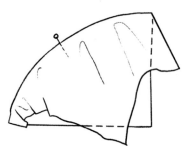

4. Repeat steps 2–3 from the pin to the other edge of the arc. With the arc still on the bottom and the now-ruffled background on top, sew along the curved edge. Press the seam allowance toward the arc. Clipping the curve is optional, but not necessary.

5. Repeat steps 1–4 for the remaining 23 arc-and-background pairs.

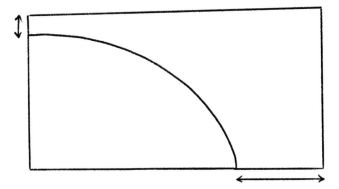

6. Trim A/AA blocks to 8½" x 4½" (21.6 x 11.4cm). The end of the curve should be 2½" (6.4cm) from the end of the background piece and the wide end of the curve should be ⅜" (1cm) from the edge of the block.

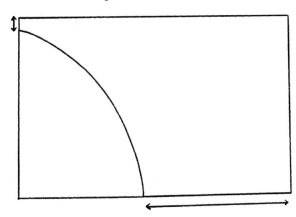

7. Trim B/BB blocks to 8½" x 5½" (21.6 x 14cm). The end of the curve should be 4½" (11.4cm) from the end of the background piece and the wide end of the curve should be ⅜" (1cm) from the edge of the block.

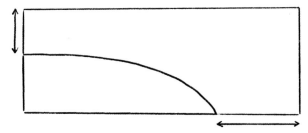

8. Trim C/CC blocks to 8½" x 3½" (21.6 x 8.9cm). The end of the curve should be 2½" (6.4cm) from the end of the background piece and the wide end of the curve should be 1½" (3.8cm) from the edge of the block.

Assembly

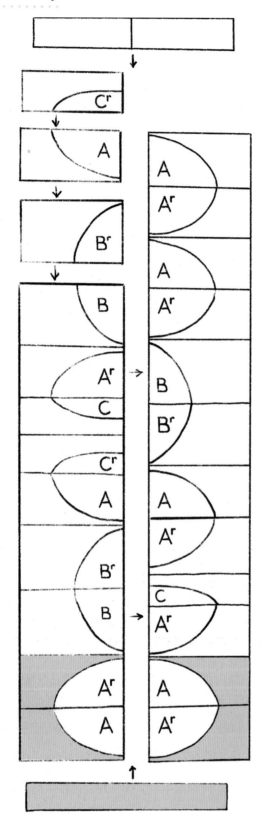

9. **Arrange blocks as in the diagram.** Sew the blocks with the purchased fabric backgrounds together in a row. Sew on the two special fabric 2 blocks for that side. Press the seams to one side.

10. **Sew the blocks with special fabric 1 together in a row.** Sew on the remaining two special fabric 2 blocks. Press the seams in the opposite direction to the row in step 9.

11. **Sew the two rows together.** Press this center seam open.

12. **Sew the top border 1 and 2 rectangles together along one short end.** Press the seam open. Sew this to the end of the table runner with the matching backgrounds (purchased fabric and special fabric 1). Press seam toward the border.

13. **Sew the bottom border rectangle to the other end of the table runner.** Press seam toward the border.

14. **Your quilt top is complete.** Layer the quilt top, batting, and backing. Quilt and bind as desired. Sew patches, nametapes, etc., back on as a final touch. Pay attention to placement.

I was very intentional when cutting the shapes for this piece. I wanted the words to be understood to convey the importance of these scrubs and the person who wore them.

Adding a Hanging Sleeve

If you would like to hang your project on the wall as art, you can add a sleeve to the back to hold a dowel.

Assembly

1. **Cut a strip of fabric 6" (16.2cm) x the width of your project.** Hem the short ends by pressing under ¼" (6mm) and then ¼" (6mm) again. Stitch down the folded edge.

2. **Fold the strip in half lengthwise, wrong sides together.** Sew using a ¼" (6mm) seam allowance. Press the strip flat with the seam positioned down the center. Press the seam open. This is your sleeve.

3. **Position the sleeve, seam side down, on the back of your quilt just below the binding.** Pin in place. With a whipstitch, hand-sew the top pressed edge of the sleeve to the back of the quilt through the backing fabric only.

4. **Fold the bottom pressed edge of the sleeve up about ¼" (6mm).** Keep the back (seam side) of the sleeve flat to the quilt. Pin in place. This makes the front of the sleeve puff out a bit to accommodate the dowel without distorting the quilt. With a whipstitch, hand-sew the bottom edge of the sleeve to the back of the quilt through the backing fabric only. Your quilt project is ready to hang!

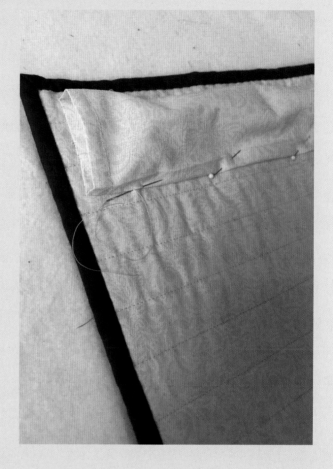

Installation

5. **Insert a dowel rod the width of your project plus 2" (5.1cm).** You can also cut down a larger rod. I like to use wood because it's easy to adjust the size and they are lightweight.

6. **Cut a piece of ribbon or string twice the width of your project.** Tie it to each end of the rod where it sticks out from the wall hanging. Check if you like the length and adjust if needed. Use hot glue or tacky glue to secure the ribbon if desired.

7. **Hang your piece from a hook or nail and enjoy!**

Variation:
Small Cairn Quilt

DIMENSIONS: 38" X 53" (96.5 X 134.6CM)

This would make a lovely small lap quilt showcasing little items, such as baby clothes. I used an army uniform and three shades of gray for a subtle look. For this version, I've given yardage for purchased background fabrics in addition to the fabrics used for the Cairn section, but a larger shirt or pants could also be pieced and used, especially for fabrics 2 and 3.

YARDAGE
(IN ADDITION TO CAIRN TABLE RUNNER)
Purchased fabric: ⅔ yard (61cm)
Special fabric 1: ⅛ yard (11.4cm)
Special fabric 2: ⅓ yard (30.5cm)
Backing: 1⅝ yards (1.5m)
Binding: ⅜ yard (34.3cm)
Batting: 42" x 57" (1.1 x 1.4m)

CUTTING
(IN ADDITION TO CAIRN TABLE RUNNER)
From purchased fabric, cut:
    (1) 20½" x 41½" (52.1 x 105.4cm) rectangle

From special fabric 1, cut:
    (1) 2½" x 41½" (6.4 x 105.4cm) strip

From special fabric 2, cut:
    (1) 20½" x 10½" (52.1 x 26.7cm) rectangle

    (1) 2½" x 10½" (6.4 x 26.7cm) rectangle

Assembly

1. Follow steps 1–13 of Cairn Table Runner (pages 92–96). You now have an assembled Cairn unit.

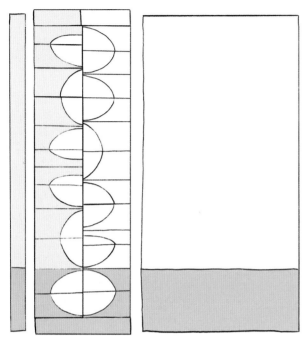

2. Sew the 2½" x 10½" (6.4 x 26.7cm) **special fabric 2 strip to the end of the special fabric 1 strip.** Press to the darker fabric. Sew the pieced fabric strip to the left side of the Cairn unit. Press toward the strip.

A Note on This Quilt

I made the Small Cairn Quilt well before the table runner. It made sense to update the quilt pattern based on the table runner, so the layout in the photo is a little different than the pattern. I used my purchased fabric and special fabric in place of special fabric 2. I also pieced the strip on the left side (larger than the strip in the updated pattern). You may choose to piece any of your larger rectangles depending on the special fabrics you are using.

3. Sew a long side of the 20½" x 10½" (52.1 x 26.7cm) **special fabric 2 rectangle to the purchased fabric rectangle.** Press to the darker fabric. Sew the pieced fabric rectangle to the right side of the Cairn unit. Press toward the rectangle.

4. Your quilt top is complete. Layer the quilt top, batting, and backing. Quilt and bind as desired. Sew patches, nametapes, etc., back on as a final touch. Pay attention to placement.

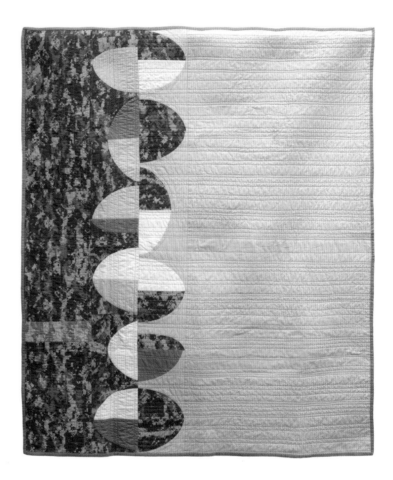

Katja's Froggy Monster

Katja's Story

Katja is an army brat. They grew up moving every three to four years, and their dad had eight deployments of varying lengths during their childhood. It was important to the family to keep ties to dad as much as possible when he wasn't at home. Through the wonders of modern technology, Katja and their brother had Skype calls when possible, and each kid had a small fabric doll with a vinyl window for a face into which they could put a picture of their dad. That doll was the inspiration for this stuffie project. No doubt, if the kids had a more huggable stuffie or a fun and practical backpack like these, it would have been treasured and much used.

Now, Katja is the one living away from home in a college dorm, so they were game for a project that was fun and a little sentimental. Katja provided one of their dad's uniforms and a couple of their own T-shirts—one from high school band and one from freshman year at college—to represent part of their life journey so far. As we collaborated on the backpack and the simple stuffie creation, we included a version with an old pair of jeans and a funky skirt picked up along Katja's travels. What emerged was a goofy, frog-like monster of huggable size, and a silly backpack version that is the perfect size to toss in snacks for a short walk in the woods or a few things for a quick trip across campus to hang out with friends. Katja's response to the result: "OMG! Squeeeee!"

Froggy-Monster Backpack

This froggy-monster backpack with a wide zipper "mouth" and an optional pocket in front is a charming gift for a little one to fill with treasures. The chunkier the zipper, the harder it will be to work with, but it is nice to use found hardware, such as the one I deconstructed from the army uniform. Make this backpack out of a parent's uniform or the household's clothing otherwise destined for the resale shop. The pocket on the front can be part of the special fabric or a separate pocket sewn onto the base fabric before assembly.

YARDAGE AND SUPPLIES

Special fabric: 1: 1½ yards (1.4m), or 1 T-shirt
Special fabric 2: 1 pant or uniform with pocket (or a pocket sewn onto any fabric)
Lining fabric: ⅓ yard (30.5cm)
Strap fabric: ¼ yard (22.9cm) fabric, or 2 yards (1.8m) of 1" (2.5cm) wide webbing
Fusible fleece: ½ yard (45.7cm)
Fusible woven interfacing (such as Shape-Flex): ½ yard (45.7cm)
Fusible heavy interfacing (such as Peltex®): ⅓ yard (30.5cm) (optional)
18" (45.7cm) zipper (or longer nonmetal zipper that will be trimmed)
Scrap felt for eyes
2 buttons for eyes (optional)
(4) 1" (2.5cm) D rings or 2 buckles
Polyester fiberfill

Download Patterns

Copy or trace pattern pieces and cut them out according to the Cutting instructions. Copy and cut dotted interfacing pieces separately. Trace around pattern pieces on the back side of your fabrics and transfer the pattern's alignment markings (notches and dots) onto the reverse side of all your pieces with a water-soluble or chalk marker.

CUTTING

From special fabric 1, cut:

  2 Head pieces

  2 Feet pieces. You could instead cut 2 pieces from special fabric 2 or lining fabric.

  2 Feet pieces, reversed. You could instead cut 2 pieces from special fabric 2 or lining fabric.

From special fabric 2, cut:

  1 Body Front piece. Place pattern so pocket is ½"–1" [1.3–2.5cm] from the top edge and centered left to right.

  1 Body Center Back piece

  1 Body Side Back piece

  1 Body Side Back piece, reversed

  1 Base piece

From lining fabric, cut:

  1 Head Base piece

  (2) 5¼" x 1" (13.3 x 2.5cm) rectangles (or width of zipper) for hinge. You could instead cut 2 rectangles from special fabric 1, or 1 rectangle from both lining and special fabric 1.

  1 Body Front piece

  1 Body Center Back piece

  1 Body Side Back piece

  1 Body Side Back piece, reversed

  1 Base piece

From strap fabric, cut:

  If using webbing: (2) 4" (10.2cm) strips

  If using webbing: (2) 20" (50.8cm) strips for kid size, or (2) 30" (76.2cm) for adult size

  If using fabric: (2) 3" (7.6cm) x WOF strips, subcut into (2) 20" (50.8cm) strips for kid size (or 30" [76.2cm] for adult size) and (2) 4" (10.2cm) strips. For sturdier straps, iron woven interfacing to back of strips.

From fusible fleece, cut (on pattern dotted lines):

  1 Body Front piece

  1 Body Center Back piece

  1 Body Side Back piece

  1 Body Side Back piece, reversed

  1 Base piece. You could instead cut this piece from heavy interfacing, which makes a firmer base, but makes it more difficult to turn the project right sides out.

From fusible woven interfacing, cut:

  2 Head pieces

  1 Head Base piece

From felt, cut:

  (2) 2" (5.1cm) diameter ovals for eyes

Zipper

Use a ⅜" (1cm) seam allowance throughout (the width of your presser foot) unless otherwise stated.

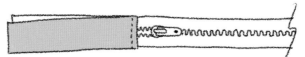

1. Prepare zipper: Sandwich the top end of the zipper between the two hinge fabric rectangles, right sides facing, with their short ends lining up with the end of the zipper. Unzip the pull tab a bit so it is out of the way. Sew through all layers. Press the hinge rectangles away from the zipper and topstitch near the seam if desired.

2. Measure the zipper 19½" (49.5cm) from the short raw end of the hinge fabrics. Mark. Bring the short end of the top hinge rectangle to the mark and pin in place.

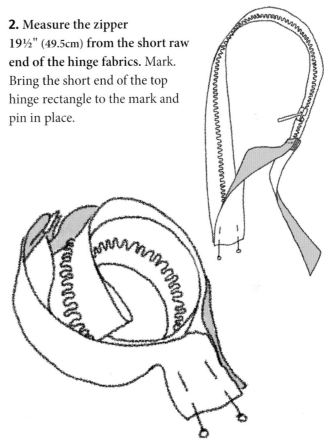

3. Turn the zipper over. Roll it up so that the bottom hinge rectangle can be brought to match the top one, right sides facing, with the zipper sandwiched in between. Pin in place and sew ⅜" (1cm) from the raw edge. Trim away excess zipper. It's okay if the zipper doesn't stay rolled up through this process. Topstitch the hinge near the seam if desired. You should now have a ring of zipper connected by two rectangles of fabric (hinge) with wrong sides together.

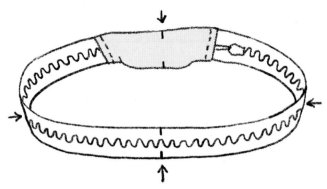

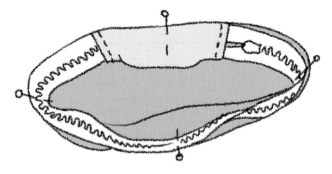

4. Mark the center of the hinge fabric near the raw edges. Fold the hinge in half at the mark. Press the ring flat to find the opposite point on the zipper and mark it. Bring the markings together and lay the ring flat again to find the opposite midpoints on the zipper; mark those. Unzip partway. Set aside.

Head

5. Fuse woven interfacing to the wrong sides the Head Base piece and Head pieces. Interfacing the Head pieces is optional depending on the fabric used. Choose one Head piece to be the front.

6. Place eye appliqués on front, using the pattern as a guide. Use a glue stick to hold felt in place. Stitch around appliqués by hand or machine. Place buttons, or smaller dark-felt circles, as desired on felt bases for a goofy look and sew in place.

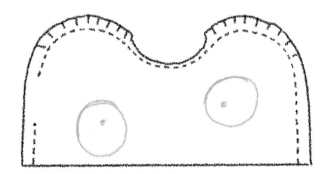

7. Place front and back Head pieces right sides together. Sew the top edge, leaving an opening for turning between marked dots. Do not sew the long bottom edge yet. Clip curves and trim the seam allowance between the "ears" to ⅛" (3mm). Press the side seams open near the bottom edge.

8. Pin the zipper ring so the pull-tab side faces the right side of the Head pieces. The Head pieces are still right sides facing. Match the center-back marking of the Head piece with the center-hinge marking. Center front to zipper center, and center side seams to zipper-midpoint marks.

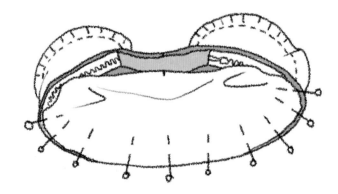

9. Place the Head Base piece right sides together with the Head pieces. Pin in place, matching notch markings and sandwiching the zipper in between. Use a zipper foot to sew around the perimeter through all layers (Head, zipper, Head Base) and at least ¼" (6mm) from the zipper edge to allow the pull-tab space to move. Turn right sides out through the opening in the Head piece seam. Leave zipper open and do not stuff yet!

Body

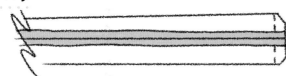

10. Make straps if using fabric: Fold each strip in half lengthwise. Sew along the long edge with a ¼" (6mm) seam allowance. Press seam allowance open and position down the center of the strip. On the long strips only, sew across one short end. Use a turning tool to turn all strips right sides out and press. Topstitch around the edges.

11. Center the fusible fleece pieces on the wrong side of their corresponding special fabric pieces. Do this for the Front, Side Back, Center Back, and Base pieces. Optionally, use the heavy interfacing on the Base piece. Fuse in place.

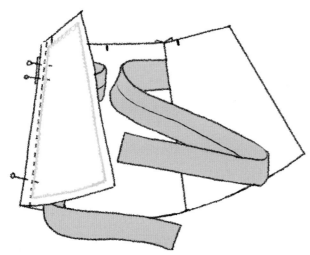

12. Pin one long strap or webbing to each side of the Center Back piece at dots. Angle the straps at 45 degrees down toward the bottom (strap seam side faces toward Center Back piece). With right sides together, sew one Side Back piece to each long side of the Center Back. Trim the strap end bit that extends beyond the seam allowance. From here on out, be careful to not sew the straps into any more seams. Press seams open.

13. Sew the opposite sides of the Side Back pieces to each side of the Front piece. Ensure right sides together. Press seams open.

14. Sew the Side Back lining pieces to each side of the Back lining piece, right sides together. Sew the opposite sides of the Side Back lining pieces to each side of the Front lining piece, leaving a 3" (7.6cm) opening in one side for turning. Press seams open.

Assembly

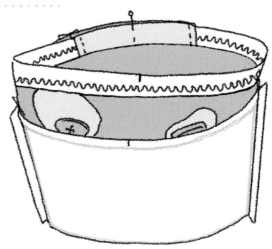

15. With the outer-body pieces wrong side out, place the Head upside down inside. The unsewn side of the zipper ring is facing up, and the pull-tab side faces the right side of the outer body. Unzip the zipper for easier maneuvering. Pin in place, matching the center-front, center-back, and side markings (these will be marked notches on the upper edge of the body, not the side back seams).

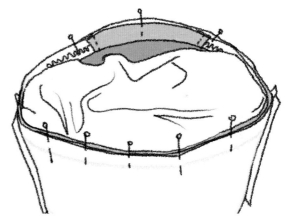

16. Place the body lining into the outer body/head, right sides facing with the zipper sandwiched between. Pin in place, matching marks. Sew around the perimeter through all layers, and at least ¼" (6mm) from the zipper edge to allow the zipper pull space to move. Turn right sides out. Press lining and outer-body fabric away from the zipper. Topstitch near the seam.

17. Make the feet: Place two feet pieces right sides together. Sew around the curved edge. Clip curve and turn right side out. Repeat with remaining two feet pieces. Stuff lightly with polyester fiberfill, keeping the feet unstuffed about 1" (2.5cm) from the opening. Pin feet to the right side of the interfaced Base piece at dots, and baste in place to secure.

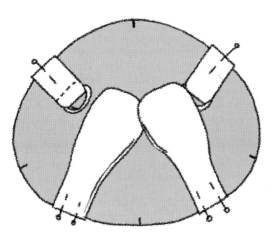

18. Thread two D rings onto each short strap piece or webbing. Fold in half to form loops. Stitch across straps or webbing close to the D rings so that they don't slip. Pin or baste the loops to the base at the Side Back seam markings.

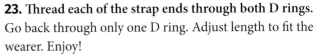

19. Turn Body inside out. Lining should be at one end and the outer body at the opposite end. Pin Base to Body, matching center-front, center-back, and side seam markings. Make sure feet and D ring loops are inside the Body. Sew around the perimeter.

20. Pin the lining Base to the lining Body, right sides together. Match center-front, center-back, and side seam markings. Sew around the perimeter.

21. Pull the backpack right side out through the opening in the lining side seam and the mouth. It's easier if you roll the Base and push one end of the roll through the side seam first, especially if you used heavy interfacing on the Base. Whipstitch the opening closed by hand. Push lining into the body. Zip up the "mouth."

22. Stuff the head as desired. Use the opening in the Head side seam. Use more stuffing for a firmer head, less for a squishy head. Whipstitch the opening closed by hand.

23. Thread each of the strap ends through both D rings. Go back through only one D ring. Adjust length to fit the wearer. Enjoy!

Variation:
Just a Stuffie

If the backpack is a more in-depth project than you want to tackle, you can easily make this froggy-monster stuffie. It still has a pocket on the front to hold special items, but now it has cute little wings instead of straps. To find the patterns used in this project, follow the QR code on page 102.

YARDAGE AND SUPPLIES

Special fabric 1: 1 T-shirt

Special fabric 2: 1 pair of pants or uniform with pocket (or a pocket sewn onto any fabric)

Fusible woven interfacing (such as Shape-Flex): ⅓ yard (30.5cm) (if necessary to stabilize head and feet fabrics)

Fusible fleece or fusible heavy interfacing (such as Peltex®): ⅓ yard (30.5cm)

Scraps of felt for eyes

2 buttons for eyes

Polyester fiberfill

CUTTING

From special fabric 1, cut:

2 Head pieces

2 Feet pieces. You could instead cut 2 pieces from special fabric 2.

2 Feet pieces, reversed. You could instead cut 2 pieces from special fabric 2.

2 Wing pieces

2 Wing pieces, reversed

From special fabric 2, cut:

1 Body Front piece. Place pattern so pocket is ½"–1" (1.3–2.5cm) from the top edge and centered left to right.

1 Body Center Back piece

1 Body Side Back piece

1 Body Side Back piece, reversed

1 Base piece

From fusible fleece, cut:

1 Base piece. You could instead cut this piece from heavy interfacing, which makes a firmer base, but makes it more difficult to turn the project right sides out.

1 Wing piece

1 Wing piece, reversed

From fusible woven interfacing, cut:

2 Head pieces

1 Wing piece

1 Wing piece, reversed

From felt, cut:

(2) 2" (5.1cm) diameter ovals for eyes

Head

Use a ⅜" (1cm) seam allowance throughout (the width of your presser foot) unless otherwise noted.

1. Fuse woven interfacing to the wrong sides of Head pieces. Choose one Head piece to be the front.

2. Place eye appliqués on front, using the pattern as a guide. Use a glue stick to hold felt in place. Stitch around appliqués by hand or machine. Place buttons, or smaller dark felt circles, as desired on felt bases for a goofy look and sew in place.

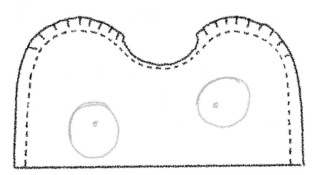

3. Place front and back Head pieces right sides together. Sew the top, curvy edge. Clip curves and trim the seam allowance between the "ears" to ⅛" (3mm). Press the side seams open near the bottom edge. Turn right sides out.

Body

4. Make wings: Iron fusible fleece to one Wing piece and one Wing piece reversed. Iron woven interfacing to the remaining two Wing pieces. Pin each fleece-fused Wing piece, right sides together, to the interfacing-fused Wing pieces. Stitch around, leaving straight base edge open for turning. Trim the curves close and clip the concave angles. Turn right sides out and press. Topstitch any wing detail as desired.

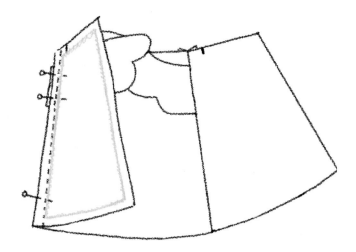

5. Pin one wing to each side of the Center Back piece at dots, each facing the center. With right sides together, sew one Side Back piece to each long side of the Center Back. From here on out, be careful to not sew the wings into any more seams.

6. Sew the opposite sides of the Side Back pieces to each side of the Front piece. Ensure right sides together. Leave a 3" (7.6cm) opening on one side for turning. Press seams open.

Assembly

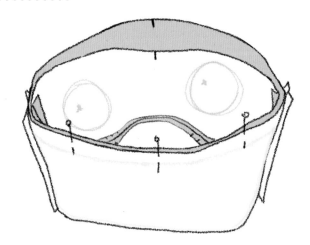

7. With the outer-body pieces wrong side out, place the Head upside down inside. Pin in place, matching the center-front, center-back, and the side markings (these will be marked notches on the upper edge of the body, not the side back seams). Sew around the perimeter.

8. Iron fusible fleece or heavy interfacing to wrong side of Base piece.

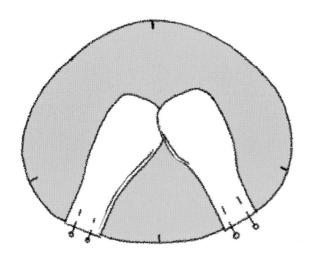

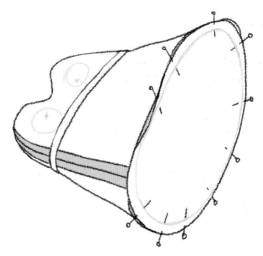

9. Make the feet: Place two feet pieces right sides together. Sew around the curved edge. Clip curve and turn right side out. Repeat with remaining two feet pieces. Stuff lightly with polyester fiberfill, keeping the feet unstuffed about 1" (2.5cm) from the opening. Pin feet to the right side of the interfaced Base piece at dots.

10. Pin Base to Body. Match center-front, center-back, and side-seam markings. Make sure feet are inside the body. Sew around the perimeter.

11. Turn right side out through the opening in the side seam. It's easier if you roll the Base and push one end of the roll through the side seam first, especially if you used heavy interfacing on the Base.

12. Stuff as desired. Use more stuffing for a firmer monster, less for a squishy one. Whipstitch the opening closed by hand.

Tanner's Patchwork

Tanner's Story

My nephew Tanner was the inspiration for this tote bag. An avid outdoorsman, he amassed a nice collection of patches from US National Parks and the Junior Ranger programs that he participated in while in elementary school. He's older now, but he still loves being outdoors, mountain biking, skiing, and hanging out with his friends as much as possible. He's got a close community that shares activities and encourages each other.

Being crafty himself, Tanner sewed his patches onto a simple canvas tote in which he carried library books and other important supplies. My sister offered up the patches for a project, but I didn't want to undo Tanner's work to give him a project that functioned basically the same way. So I used his idea as a jumping-off point and created a tote bag that can be made of repurposed clothing, such as scout uniforms or outgrown jeans—a memento for a kid, or a parent, of a special period during childhood. It also helps keep a bit of outgrown clothing out of landfills, which anyone concerned about the environment (like Tanner) can appreciate. The project would be appropriate not only for patches, but also pins, which are popular to collect for kids and grown-ups alike. The large pockets inside protect the pin backs so that they are not snagged by the bag contents.

As I was making the Tanner-inspired outdoors version, I also thought about using the tote as a project bag for makers—especially those who knit, crochet, or hand-piece quilts—who need a way to transport individual project supplies to community get-togethers (like Tanner did) and collect fun pins and patches from shop hops and sew-a-longs. The idea of combining meaningful fabrics with meaningful collectibles into a practical object appeals to the crafty, the thrifty, and the sentimental in all of us.

Patchwork Tote

A tote is a fun way to show off one's collection of pins and patches. Inside each side is a pocket to hide and protect pin backs. Choose long or short carrying handles to fit your preference.

Assembly

Use a ⅜" (1cm) seam allowance throughout.

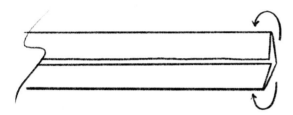

1. Fold lining handle strips in half lengthwise. Press to create crease. Open up, fold long edges to the center crease, and press again. Fold in half lengthwise and press. You will have four layers with the long raw edges enclosed. Topstitch close to the long edges to finish the handles.

2. Optional: Pin a special fabric strip down the center of each handle. Stitch down the center using a wide zigzag or decorative stitch. Fray the long edges for texture.

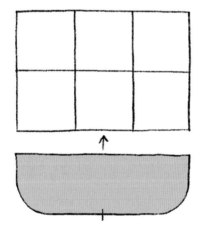

3. Make the front: Arrange six 5" x 5" (12.7 x 12.7cm) squares in two rows of three. Sew the first row together, then the second. Press seam allowances open and sew the two rows together. Sew a 5" x 13¾" (12.7 x 34.9cm) rectangle to the six-square unit. If working with denim or another fabric that frays attractively, sew the squares with wrong sides together so the seam allowances are on the outside. Repeat for the back.

YARDAGE

Special fabric: 3 pants or other garments for a variety of color
Lining fabric: 1½ yards (1.4m)
Woven interfacing: 1⅝ yards (1.5m)
Stiff interfacing: 11" x 4" (27.9 x 10.2cm) for the base
(2) 11" (27.9cm) sew-on hook-and-loop tape strips

CUTTING

From at least two special fabrics (1 and 2), cut:
  (16) 5" x 5" (12.7 x 12.7cm) squares

From contrasting special fabric 3, cut:
  (2) 5" x 13¾" (12.7 x 34.9cm) rectangles for the front and back

  (1) 5" x 20½" (12.7 x 52.1cm) rectangle for the base

  Optional: (2) 1" x 32" (2.5 x 81.3cm) strips for long handles, or
  (2) 1" x 18" (2.5 x 45.7cm) for short handles

From lining fabric, cut:
  (4) 13¾" x 13¾" (34.9 x 34.9cm) squares for the front, back, front pocket, and back pocket

  (4) 5" x 9¼" (12.7 x 23.5cm) rectangles for the sides and side pockets

  (1) 5" x 20½" (12.7 x 52.1cm) rectangle for the base

  (2) 5" x 32" (12.7 x 81.3cm) strips for long handles, or
  (2) 5" x 18" (12.7 x 45.7cm) for short handles

From woven interfacing, cut:
  (2) 13¾" x 13¾" (34.9 x 34.9cm) squares for front and back

  (2) 13¾" x 12¾" (34.9 x 32.4cm) rectangles for the large pockets

  (2) 1" x 5" (2.5 x 12.7cm) strips for the side pocket hems

4. Draw a curve at each bottom corner of the side rectangles. Use the corner template (follow QR code on page 102). Cut on the drawn line to create curved corners. Sew on any patches now. Mark the center bottom on both the front piece and the back unit.

5. For the sides, sew two 5" x 5" (12.7 x 12.7cm) squares together. Repeat with the two remaining squares. Mark the center of the long edges of the base rectangle. Sew a pair of squares to each end. Center the 11" x 4" (27.9 x 10.2cm) stiff interfacing on the reverse side of the base and fuse in place.

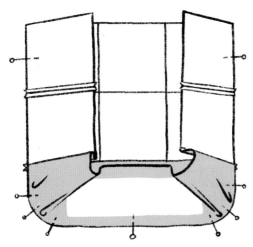

6. Pin one long side of the side/base strip to the front unit, right sides together. Match the ends of the side strip to the upper-left and upper-right corners of the front unit. Match center-bottom markings. Match the seams of the 5" x 5" (12.7 x 12.7cm) squares. Add more pins as necessary around the curved corners. Sew the side/base strip to the front unit. Clip corner curves and press seam allowance toward the side strip. Repeat to add the back piece to the other long edge of the side/base strip, pressing as best as possible.

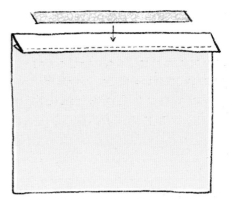

7. Make the large pockets: Fuse the two 13¾" x 12½" (34.9 x 32.4cm) rectangles of woven stabilizer to two 13¾" x 13¾" (34.9 x 34.9cm) pocket squares, leaving the top 1" (2.5cm) unstabilized. Fold the unstabilized edge of the pocket pieces over 1" (2.5cm) and press. Fold and press again. Topstitch each piece close to the first fold. Center the hook-half of the hook-and-loop tape over the folded pocket tops on the reverse side of each pocket piece, and stitch in place.

8. Make the front and back lining: Fuse the two 13¾" x 13¾" (34.9 x 34.9cm) squares of woven stabilizer to the two lining squares. Place the loop-half of the hook-and-loop tape 2¼" (5.7cm) down from the top edge of each lining piece on the right side, and stitch in place.

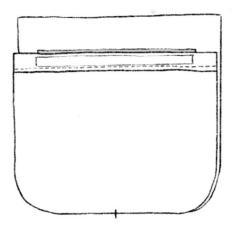

9. Pin a large pocket piece over the front lining piece, both pieces right sides up. Line up the side and bottom edges, making sure the hook-and-loop tape strips are aligned and sealed. Mark the bottom two corners with the corner template, and cut the rounded corners through both layers. Mark the center of the bottom edge with a pin through both layers. Repeat for the other pocket piece and the back lining piece.

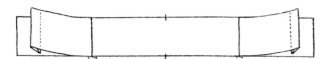

10. Make the sides: Fuse a 1" x 5" (2.5 x 12.7cm) strip of interfacing to the wrong side of one short end of a 5" x 9¼" (12.7 x 23.5cm) rectangle. Fold the fused section over and press. Fold again to encase the raw edge and press. Topstitch in place. Repeat on a second rectangle. These are your side pockets. Place the side pocket pieces on top of the remaining two side rectangles, right sides up. Pin together. Sew one of these pairs to each short end of the base rectangle, right sides together.

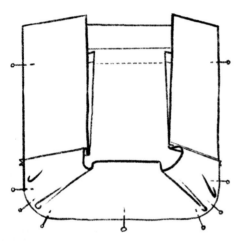

11. Mark the center of the base rectangle. Pin one long side of the side/base lining to one of the large-pocket lining units, right sides together. Match the ends of the side strip to the upper-left and upper-right corners of the large lining unit. Match center-bottom markings. Add more pins as necessary around the curved corners. Sew the side/base strip to the large lining unit. Clip corner curves and press seam allowance toward the side strip. Repeat to add the other large-pocket lining unit to the other long edge of the side/base strip, pressing as best as possible.

12. Pin the handle ends to the top, raw edge of the front and back units. Ensure right sides together and the handles are not twisted.

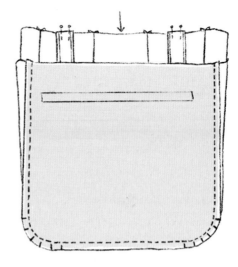

13. Insert outer bag into bag lining, right sides together. Pin the top, raw edges together. Make sure handles are down in the bag area and away from the raw edges. Sew edges together with a ⅜" (1cm) seam allowance, leaving a 4" (10.2cm) opening between the handles on the back side for turning. Turn bag right sides out through hole. Press. Topstitch close to top edge of bag to finish and close turning hole.

14. Attach any pins through the outer bag and lining. Place so the pin backs are protected inside the large pockets. Close the hook and loop strips. Enjoy your new tote bag!

Gallery

The wonderful thing about memory quilts and other items made from sentimental clothing is that everyone's projects will be unique. In this gallery, you'll see variations of the projects in this book that show how the same pattern can look using different fabrics. Compare the Scrappy Star Quilt made of light-colored shirts to Mike's Star Quilt with its solid-fabric background. Or Ralph's Square Dance Quilt with its similar-colored T-shirts compared to Tanner's flannel-shirt version, which shows off the way matching a Log Cabin fabric to the adjacent solid-block fabric breaks up the strict grid of the quilt. I hope these examples will inspire you and help you to visualize how your special fabrics might be used to quilt your unique story.

Mike's Star Quilt

Tanner's Forest Square Dance

Angela's Wonky Star

Art's HST Tie Pillows

Rust-Colored Pathway

Other Eden's Portal

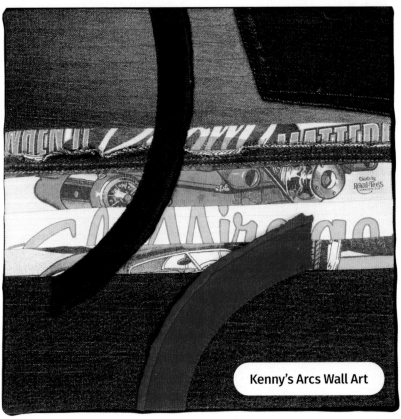

Kenny's Arcs Wall Art

Index

Note: Page numbers in *italics* indicate projects. Page numbers in **bold** indicate Gallery items.

accent color, 10–11
Angela's Aspens, *68–71*
Angela's Wonky Stars, **116**
Anvil Star Pillow, *37–41*
Arc blocks, 94–96
Arcs Wall Art, *79–80*, **118**
art, wall. *See* memory projects, Constanze's
  Textile Art
Art's Portal, 84, *86–89*
Aspens Quilt, *70–71*

backpack, Froggy-Monster, *102–6*. *See also* tote,
  patchwork
basting, 25–27
batting, defined, 22
bias, defined, 22
binding, 22, 29
blocks, 22, 24
border, defined, 22
border measurements, 53

cairn quilt, small (*var.*), *98–99*
Cairn Table Runner, *92–97*
canvas, mounting on, 85
chain piecing, 24
chalk, for marking, 21
color
  accent, adding, 10–11
  contrast, sorting by, 10
  sorting fabric by, 9–10
Constanze's Textile Art. *See* memory projects
contrast, sorting by, 10
couching stitch, 82
curved pieces, 94–96. *See also* Arcs Wall Art
cutters, rotary, 20
cutting, fussy, 50. *See also* deconstructing
  clothing

deconstructing clothing, 12–16
  general guidelines and notes, 12
  identifying elements to highlight, 12
  marking seam allowance, 14
  off-center cuts, 14
  order of operations, 13
  other garments, 16
  pants, 15
  placket use and, 64
  rectangle or strip cuts, 14
  rough cutting, 13, 14
  shirts, 13–15
delicate fabric, 18, 19

Eden's Cairn. *See* memory projects
Eden's Portal, **118**

embroidery thread, 21
enders, leaders and, 23

fabric. *See also* deconstructing clothing
  delicate or stretchy, 18, 19
  interfacing application, 18
  non-rectangular detail prep, 70
  organizing and color choices, 9–11
  prepping (delicate, medium-weight, stretchy),
    12–13, 18, 70
  sorting by color, 9–10
  sorting by contrast, 10
  sorting by type, 9
  stabilizers, 19
  yardage uses, 17
Flying Geese, 70–71, 76–78
Froggy-Monster Backpack, *102–6*

Gallery, **115–18**
glossary of terms, 22
glue, 21
grain, defined, 22
Grow Wall Art, *81–82*

hand quilting, 27–28
hanging sleeve, adding, 97
Hearth Wall Art, *76–78*
HST (Half-Square Triangles), 22, 25, 71, **117**
HST Throw Pillow, *54–55*, **117**

interfacing, adding to fabric, 18
iron and ironing board, 20. *See also* pressing
  cloth

Joni's Pathway, *60–67*, **117**
Just a Stuffie (*var.*), *107–9*

Katja's Froggy Monster. *See* memory projects
Kenny's Arcs Wall Art, **118**
Kenny's Stripes, *56–59*

leaders and enders, 23
Log Cabin, 76–78
Log Cabin (blocks), 34–35, 42–43, 46–47
Log Star Pillow, *34*
longarm quilting, 28

machine feet, 20. *See also* walking foot
markers, fabric, 21
measurements, border, 53
measuring supplies, 20, 21
memory projects
  about: overview of, 30

Angela's Aspens, *68–71*; about: Angela's story,
  68; Aspens Quilt, *70–71*; Wonky Star, **116**
Art's Portal, *86–89*; about: Art's story, 84, 86;
  Portal Quilt, *88–89*
Constanze's Textile Art, *72–85* (*See also* Art's
  Portal); about: Constanze's story, 72; Arcs
  Wall Art, *79–80*; Flock Wall Art, *74–75*;
  Grow Wall Art, *81–82*; Hearth Wall Art,
  76–78; Waterfall Wall Art, *83–84*
Eden's Cairn, *90–99*; about: Eden's story,
  90–91; Cairn Table Runner, *92–97*; Small
  Cairn Quilt (*var.*), *98–99*
Gregory's Wonky Stars, *48–55*; about: Greg's
  story, 48; HST Throw Pillow, *54–55*; Wonky
  Star, *50–53*
Joni's Pathway, *60–67*, **117**; about: Joni's story,
  60; Pathway Table Runner, *62–65*; Patio
  Pillow (*var.*), *66–67*
Katja's Froggy Monster, *100–109*; about:
  Katja's story, 100; Froggy-Monster Backpack,
  102–6; Just a Stuffie (*var.*), *107–9*
Kenny's Stripes, *56–59*; about: Kenny's story,
  56; Stripes Quilt, *58–59*
Mike's Stars, *32–43*, **115**; about: Mike's story,
  32; Anvil Star Pillow, *37–41*; Log Star Pillow,
  34; Sawtooth Star Pillow, *38–39*; Scrappy
  Star Quilt (*var.*), *42–43*
Ralph's Square Dance, *44–47*; about: Ralph's
  story, 44; Square Dance Quilt, *46–47*
Tanner's Patchwork, *110–14*; about: Tanner's
  story, 110; Forest Square Dance, **116**;
  Patchwork Tote, *112–14*
memory quilts
  about: getting started, 8
  appeal of, 6
  noting what colors to use where, 11
  organizing and color choices, 9–11
  preparing fabric, 12–13, 18, 70
  sorting fabric by color, contrast, and type,
    9–10
Mike's Stars. *See* memory projects
mounting on canvas, 85

needles, sewing machine, 20
nesting seams, 24–25

pants, deconstructing, 15
Patchwork Tote, *112–14*
Pathway Table Runner, *62–65*
Patio Pillow (*var.*), *66–67*
pencil, 21
piecing, defined, 22
pillows
  about: pillow backs, 40–41

Anvil Star Pillow, *37–41*
HST Throw Pillow, *54–55*, **117**
Log Star Pillow, *34*
Patio Pillow (var.), *66–67*
Sawtooth Star Pillow, *38–39*
pin basting, 26
pins, straight, 21
plackets, for strips, 64
Portal Quilt, *88–89*
prepping fabric, 12–13, 18, 70
pressing cloth, 21
projects. *See* memory projects

quilt sandwich, defined, 22
quilt top, defined, 22
quilting
    about: overview of, 27
    defined, 22, 27
    hand, 27–28
    longarm, 28
    machines for, 27, 28
    straight-line, with walking foot, 27
    techniques, 27–28
quilts, defined, 22

Ralph's Square Dance, *44–47*
rotary cutters, 20
rotary mat, 21
rotary ruler, 20
rough cutting, 13, 14
ruler, rotary, 20
rulers, 20, 21

sashing, defined, 22
Sawtooth Star Pillow, *38–39*
scissors, 21
Scrappy Star Quilt (*var.*), *42–43*
seam rippers, 21
seam(s)
    allowances, 14, 23
    defined, 22
    nesting, 24–25
self-healing rotary mat, 21
selvage, defined, 22
sewing. *See also* quilting; techniques
    binding, 22, 29
    seam allowance, 14, 23
    supplies, 20–21
    terms and definitions, 22
sewing machine and accessories/supplies, 20
sewing machine needle, 20
shirts
    deconstructing, 13–15
    ways to use (front, patchwork, etc.), 17
Square Dance Quilt, *46–47*
Star Points, 35–36, 37, 38, 43
straight pins, 21
stretchy fabric, 18, 19
stripes, straight, 58. *See also* Kenny's Stripes
strips
    plackets for, 64
    strip cuts, 14
supplies, sewing, 20–21

table runners, *62–65*, *92–97*
Tanner's Patchwork, *110–14*, **116**

techniques. *See also* quilting
    basting, 25–27
    binding, 22, 29
    blocks, 24
    chain piecing, 24
    couching stitch, 82
    HST (Half-Square Triangles), 22, 25
    leaders and enders, 23
    nesting seams, 24–25
    seam allowance, 14, 23
    "twirling" intersections, 25
    units, 24
template, defined, 22
terms and definitions, 22
thread
    basting, 26–27
    embroidery, 21
    quality importance, 20
tote, patchwork, *112–14*. *See also* backpack, Froggy-Monster
triangles, half square (HST), 22, 25
"twirling" intersections, 25

units, 24

walking foot, 20, 27
wall art. *See* memory projects, Constanze's Textile Art
wall hanging, adding sleeve for, 97
Waterfall Wall Art, *83–84*
WOF (width of fabric), 22
Wonky Star, **116**. *See also* memory projects, Gregory's Wonky Stars

About the Author

Kristin La Flamme has always been artistic, having learned how to sew at an early age. She pursued many art forms and focused on graphic design in college. When introduced to quilting after marrying into a family of quilters, she took to the craft easily, given her creative background. Kristin found quilting to be an exciting outlet that combined the same elements of color, shape, and pattern she had been drawn to in graphic design.

She has now been making and exhibiting art quilts for several decades. They always have a narrative, whether expressing yearning for a home with roots, the experiences of an army wife, or remembrance, such as the quilts for the Social Justice Sewing Academy. The fabrics she chooses add to the meaning of the finished piece. Making memory quilts is similar in that they carry the story of the person or event being honored. In her day job as a fabric coordinator at a sewing center, Kristin finds customers often ask her for tips on designing and creating T-shirt quilts and other memory quilts. Her experience working with a variety of fabrics, and years of creating her own designs, has been helpful in guiding customers and sharing resources. The path to this book has been winding, but here it is with the hope that it will provide inspiration and guidance for makers.

Kristin has settled in Portland, Oregon, where she and her husband enjoy finally being in the same time zone as their extended family.